Simple Air Fryer Cookbook

Easy Recipes for Beginners with Tips & Tricks to Fry, Grill, Roast, and Bake

Joan Sewell

Contents

INTRODUCTION

Do you crave fried food but worry that takeout is unhealthy?

Are you ready to maintain your original weight while savoring crispy treats?

Do you want to wow your family, friends and even yourself with new delicious air fryer recipes?

Here's your compass to start your journey to air fryer simplicity - Simple Air Fryer Cookbook!

This cookbook is full of useful content and tasty recipes:

Air fryer tips & tricks

Easy instruction on how to clean the air fryer

Time table for every type of food

Plenty of poultry, pork, and beef recipes

Easy snacks and bread

Healthy vegetable meals and side dishes

Quick breakfast recipes for the whole family

Extra delicious no-fuss desserts

The recipes are clear and easy to follow, even for a beginner. You DON'T have to spend much time cooking because you can make a delicious meal for the whole family in just 30 minutes!

Get it now and do yourself a big favor! Get the best air fryer recipes and you will love it!

Bread And Breakfast
Spinach-bacon Rollups

Servings: 4
Cooking Time: 9 Minutes
Ingredients:

- 4 flour tortillas (6- or 7-inch size)
- 4 slices Swiss cheese
- 1 cup baby spinach leaves
- 4 slices turkey bacon

Directions:

1. Preheat air fryer to 390°F.
2. On each tortilla, place one slice of cheese and ¼ cup of spinach.
3. Roll up tortillas and wrap each with a strip of bacon. Secure each end with a toothpick.
4. Place rollups in air fryer basket, leaving a little space in between them.
5. Cook for 4minutes. Turn and rearrange rollups (for more even cooking) and cook for 5minutes longer, until bacon is crisp.

Orange Trail Oatmeal

Servings: 4
Cooking Time: 20 Minutes
Ingredients:

- 1 ½ cups quick-cooking oats
- 1/3 cup light brown sugar
- 1 egg
- 1 tsp orange zest
- 1 tbsp orange juice
- 2 tbsp whole milk
- 2 tbsp honey
- 2 tbsp butter, melted
- 2 tsp dried cranberries
- 1 tsp dried blueberries
- 1/8 tsp ground nutmeg
- Salt to taste
- ¼ cup pecan pieces

Directions:

1. Preheat air fryer at 325ºF. Combine the oats, sugar, egg, orange zest, orange juice, milk, honey, butter, dried cranberries, dried blueberries, nutmeg, salt, and pecan in a bowl. Press mixture into a greased cake pan. Place cake pan in the frying basket and Roast for 8 minutes. Let cool onto for 5 minutes before slicing. Serve.

Fry Bread

Servings: 4
Cooking Time: 5 Minutes
Ingredients:

- 1 cup flour
- 2 teaspoons baking powder
- ¼ teaspoon salt
- ¼ cup lukewarm milk
- 1 teaspoon oil-
- 2–3 tablespoons water
- oil for misting or cooking spray

Directions:

1. Stir together flour, baking powder, and salt. Gently mix in the milk and oil. Stir in 1 tablespoon water. If needed, add more water 1 tablespoon at a time until stiff dough forms. Dough shouldn't be sticky, so use only as much as you need.

2. Divide dough into 4 portions and shape into balls. Cover with a towel and let rest for 10minutes.

3. Preheat air fryer to 390°F.

4. Shape dough as desired:

5. a. Pat into 3-inch circles. This will make a thicker bread to eat plain or with a sprinkle of cinnamon or honey butter. You can cook all 4 at once.

6. b. Pat thinner into rectangles about 3 x 6 inches. This will create a thinner bread to serve as a base for dishes such as Indian tacos. The circular shape is more traditional, but rectangles allow you to cook 2 at a time in your air fryer basket.

7. Spray both sides of dough pieces with oil or cooking spray.

8. Place the 4 circles or 2 of the dough rectangles in the air fryer basket and cook at 390°F for 3minutes. Spray tops, turn, spray other side, and cook for 2 more minutes. If necessary, repeat to cook remaining bread.

9. Serve piping hot as is or allow to cool slightly and add toppings to create your own Native American tacos.

Canadian Bacon & Cheese Sandwich

Servings: 1
Cooking Time: 30 Minutes
Ingredients:

- 1 English muffin, halved
- 1 egg
- 1 Canadian bacon slice
- 1 slice provolone cheese

Directions:

1. Preheat air fryer to 350°F. Put the muffin, crusty side up, in the frying basket. Place a slice of bacon next to the muffins and Bake for 5 minutes. Flip the bacon and muffins, and lay a slice of provolone cheese on top of the muffins. Beat the egg in a small heatproof bowl.

2. Add the bowl in the frying basket next to the bacon and muffins and Bake for 15 minutes, or until the cheese melts, bacon is crispy and eggs set. Remove the muffin to a plate, layer a slice of bacon, then the egg and top with the second toasted muffin.

Baked Eggs With Bacon-tomato Sauce

Servings: 1
Cooking Time: 12 Minutes
Ingredients:

- 1 teaspoon olive oil
- 2 tablespoons finely chopped onion
- 1 teaspoon chopped fresh oregano
- pinch crushed red pepper flakes
- 1 (14-ounce) can crushed or diced tomatoes
- salt and freshly ground black pepper
- 2 slices of bacon, chopped
- 2 large eggs
- ¼ cup grated Cheddar cheese
- fresh parsley, chopped

Directions:

1. Start by making the tomato sauce. Preheat a medium saucepan over medium heat on the stovetop. Add the olive oil and sauté the onion, oregano and pepper flakes for 5 minutes. Add the tomatoes and bring to a simmer. Season with salt and freshly ground black pepper and simmer for 10 minutes.

2. Meanwhile, Preheat the air fryer to 400°F and pour a little water into the bottom of the air fryer drawer. (This will help prevent the grease that drips into the bottom drawer from burning and smoking.) Place the bacon in the air fryer basket and air-fry at 400°F for 5 minutes, shaking the basket every once in a while.

3. When the bacon is almost crispy, remove it to a paper-towel lined plate and rinse out the air fryer drawer, draining away the bacon grease.

4. Transfer the tomato sauce to a shallow 7-inch pie dish. Crack the eggs on top of the sauce and scatter the cooked bacon back on top. Season with salt and freshly ground black pepper and transfer the pie dish into the air fryer basket. You can use an aluminum foil sling to help with this by taking a long piece of aluminum foil, folding it in half lengthwise twice until it is roughly 26-inches by 3-inches. Place this under the pie dish and hold the ends of the foil to move the pie dish in and out of the air fryer basket. Tuck the ends of the foil beside the pie dish while it cooks in the air fryer.

5. Air-fry at 400°F for 5 minutes, or until the eggs are almost cooked to your liking. Sprinkle cheese on top and air-fry for an additional 2 minutes. When the cheese has melted, remove the pie dish from the air fryer, sprinkle with a little chopped parsley and let the eggs cool for a few minutes – just enough time to toast some buttered bread in your air fryer!

All-in-one Breakfast Toast

Servings: 1
Cooking Time: 10 Minutes
Ingredients:

- 1 strip of bacon, diced
- 1 slice of 1-inch thick bread (such as Texas Toast or hand-sliced bread)
- 1 tablespoon softened butter (optional)
- 1 egg
- salt and freshly ground black pepper
- ¼ cup grated Colby or Jack cheese

Directions:

1. Preheat the air fryer to 400°F.
2. Air-fry the bacon for 3 minutes, shaking the basket once or twice while it cooks. Remove the bacon to a paper towel lined plate and set aside.
3. Use a sharp paring knife to score a large circle in the middle of the slice of bread, cutting halfway through, but not all the way through to the cutting board. Press down on the circle in the center of the bread slice to create an indentation. If using, spread the softened butter on the edges and in the hole of the bread.
4. Transfer the slice of bread, hole side up, to the air fryer basket. Crack the egg into the center of the bread, and season with salt and pepper.
5. Air-fry at 380°F for 5 minutes. Sprinkle the grated cheese around the edges of the bread leaving the center of the yolk uncovered, and top with the cooked bacon. Press the cheese and bacon into the bread lightly to help anchor it to the bread and prevent it from blowing around in the air fryer.
6. Air-fry for one or two more minutes (depending on how you like your egg cooked), just to melt the cheese and finish cooking the egg. Serve immediately.

Vegetarian Quinoa Cups

Servings: 6
Cooking Time: 25 Minutes
Ingredients:

- 1 carrot, chopped
- 1 zucchini, chopped
- 4 asparagus, chopped
- ¾ cup quinoa flour
- 2 tbsp lemon juice
- ¼ cup nutritional yeast
- ¼ tsp garlic powder
- Salt and pepper to taste

Directions:

1. Preheat air fryer to 340°F. Combine the vegetables, quinoa flour, water, lemon juice, nutritional yeast, garlic powder, salt, and pepper in a medium bowl, and mix well.Divide the mixture between 6 cupcake molds. Place the filled molds into the air fryer and Bake for 20 minutes, or until the tops are lightly browned and a toothpick inserted into the center comes out clean. Serve cooled.

Cheddar & Sausage Tater Tots

Servings: 4
Cooking Time: 25 Minutes
Ingredients:

- 12 oz ground chicken sausage
- 4 eggs
- 1 cup sour cream
- 1 tsp Worcestershire sauce
- 1 tsp shallot powder
- Salt and pepper to taste
- 1 lb frozen tater tots
- ¾ cup grated cheddar

Directions:

1. Whisk eggs, sour cream, Worcestershire sauce and shallot in a bowl. Add salt and pepper to taste. Coat a skillet with cooking spray. Over medium heat, brown the ground sausage for 3-4 minutes. Break larger pieces with a spoon or spatula. Set aside.
2. Preheat air fryer to 330°F. Prepare a baking pan with a light spray of cooking oil. Layer the bottom of the pan with tater tots, then place in the air fryer. Bake for 6 minutes, then shake the pan. Cover tater tots with cooked sausage and egg mixture. Continue cooking for 6 minutes. Top with cheese, then cook for another 2-3 minutes or until cheese is melted. Serve warm.

Classic Cinnamon Rolls

Servings: 4
Cooking Time: 6 Minutes
Ingredients:

- 1½ cups all-purpose flour
- 1 tablespoon granulated sugar
- 2 teaspoons baking powder
- ½ teaspoon salt
- 4 tablespoons butter, divided
- ½ cup buttermilk
- 2 tablespoons brown sugar
- 1 teaspoon cinnamon
- 1 cup powdered sugar
- 2 tablespoons milk

Directions:

1. Preheat the air fryer to 360°F.
2. In a large bowl, stir together the flour, sugar, baking powder, and salt. Cut in 3 tablespoons of the butter with a pastry blender or two knives until coarse crumbs remain. Stir in the buttermilk until a dough forms.
3. Place the dough onto a floured surface and roll out into a square shape about ½ inch thick.
4. Melt the remaining 1 tablespoon of butter in the microwave for 20 seconds. Using a pastry brush or your fingers, spread the melted butter onto the dough.
5. In a small bowl, mix together the brown sugar and cinnamon. Sprinkle the mixture across the surface of the dough. Roll the dough up, forming a long log. Using a pastry cutter or sharp knife, cut 10 cinnamon rolls.
6. Carefully place the cinnamon rolls into the air fryer basket. Then bake at 360°F for 6 minutes or until golden brown.
7. Meanwhile, in a small bowl, whisk together the powdered sugar and milk.
8. Plate the cinnamon rolls and drizzle the glaze over the surface before serving.

Holiday Breakfast Casserole

Servings:2
Cooking Time: 25 Minutes
Ingredients:

- ¼ cup cooked spicy breakfast sausage
- 5 eggs
- 2 tbsp heavy cream
- ½ tsp ground cumin
- Salt and pepper to taste
- ½ cup feta cheese crumbles
- 1 tomato, diced
- 1 can green chiles, including juice
- 1 zucchini, diced

Directions:

1. Preheat air fryer to 325ºF. Mix all ingredients in a bowl and pour into a greased baking pan. Place the pan in the frying basket and Bake for 14 minutes. Let cool for 5 minutes before slicing. Serve right away.

Zucchini Hash Browns

Servings: 4
Cooking Time: 20 Minutes
Ingredients:

- 2 shredded zucchinis
- 2 tbsp nutritional yeast
- 1 tsp allspice
- 1 egg white

Directions:

1. Preheat air fryer to 400°F. Combine zucchinis, nutritional yeast, allspice, and egg white in a bowl. Make 4 patties out of the mixture. Cut 4 pieces of parchment paper, put a patty on each foil, and fold in all sides to create a rectangle. Using a spatula, flatten them and spread them.

2. Then unwrap each foil and remove the hash browns onto the fryer and Air Fry for 12 minutes until golden brown and crispy, turning once. Serve right away.

Honey Donuts

Servings: 6
Cooking Time: 25 Minutes + Chilling Time
Ingredients:

- 1 refrigerated puff pastry sheet
- 2 tsp flour
- 2 ½ cups powdered sugar
- 3 tbsp honey
- 2 tbsp milk
- 2 tbsp butter, melted
- ½ tsp vanilla extract
- ½ tsp ground cinnamon
- Pinch of salt

Directions:

1. Preheat the air fryer to 325°F. Dust a clean work surface with flour and lay the puff pastry on it, then cut crosswise into five 3-inch wide strips. Cut each strip into thirds for 15 squares. Lay round parchment paper in the bottom of the basket, then add the pastry squares in a single layer.

2. Make sure none are touching. Bake for 13-18 minutes or until brown, then leave on a rack to cool. Repeat for all dough. Combine the sugar, honey, milk, butter, vanilla, cinnamon, and salt in a small bowl and mix with a wire whisk until combined. Dip the top half of each donut in the glaze, turn the donut glaze side up, and return to the wire rack. Let cool until the glaze sets, then serve.

Banana Bread

Servings: 6
Cooking Time: 20 Minutes
Ingredients:

- cooking spray
- 1 cup white wheat flour
- ½ teaspoon baking powder
- ¼ teaspoon salt
- ¼ teaspoon baking soda
- 1 egg
- ½ cup mashed ripe banana
- ¼ cup plain yogurt
- ¼ cup pure maple syrup
- 2 tablespoons coconut oil
- ½ teaspoon pure vanilla extract

Directions:

1. Preheat air fryer to 330°F.
2. Lightly spray 6 x 6-inch baking dish with cooking spray.
3. In a medium bowl, mix together the flour, baking powder, salt, and soda.
4. In a separate bowl, beat the egg and add the mashed banana, yogurt, syrup, oil, and vanilla. Mix until well combined.
5. Pour liquid mixture into dry ingredients and stir gently to blend. Do not beat. Batter may be slightly lumpy.
6. Pour batter into baking dish and cook at 330°F for 20 minutes or until toothpick inserted in center of loaf comes out clean.

Cherry-apple Oatmeal Cups

Servings: 2
Cooking Time: 20 Minutes
Ingredients:

- 2/3 cup rolled oats
- 1 cored apple, diced
- 4 pitted cherries, diced
- ½ tsp ground cinnamon
- ¾ cup milk

Directions:

1. Preheat air fryer to 350°F. Mix the oats, apple, cherries, and cinnamon in a heatproof bowl. Add in milk and Bake for 6 minutes, stir well and Bake for 6 more minutes until the fruit are soft. Serve cooled.

Crispy Samosa Rolls

Servings: 4
Cooking Time: 30 Minutes
Ingredients:

- 2/3 cup canned peas
- 4 scallions, finely sliced
- 2 cups grated potatoes
- 2 tbsp lemon juice
- 1 tsp ground ginger
- 1 tsp curry powder
- 1 tsp Garam masala
- ¼ cup chickpea flour
- 1 tbsp tahini
- 8 rice paper wrappers

Directions:

1. Preheat air fryer to 350°F. Mix the peas, scallions, potatoes, lemon juice, ginger, curry powder, Garam masala, and chickpea flour in a bowl. In another bowl, whisk tahini and 1/3 cup of water until combined. Set aside on a plate.
2. Submerge the rice wrappers, one by one, into the tahini mixture until they begin to soften and set aside on a plate.
3. Fill each wrap with 1/3 cup of the veggie mixture and wrap them into a roll. Bake for 15 minutes until golden brown and crispy, turning once. Serve right away.

16

Eggless Mung Bean Tart

Servings: 2
Cooking Time: 20 Minutes
Ingredients:

- 2 tsp soy sauce
- 1 tsp lime juice
- 1 large garlic clove, minced or pressed
- ½ tsp red chili flakes
- ½ cup mung beans, soaked
- Salt and pepper to taste
- ½ minced shallot
- 1 green onion, chopped

Directions:

1. Preheat the air fryer to 390°F. Add the soy sauce, lime juice, garlic, and chili flakes to a bowl and stir. Set aside.Place the drained beans in a blender along with ½ cup of water, salt, and pepper. Blend until smooth. Stir in shallot and green onion, but do not blend.
2. Pour the batter into a greased baking pan. Bake for 15 minutes in the air fryer until golden. A knife inserted in the center should come out clean. Once cooked, cut the "quiche" into quarters. Drizzle with sauce and serve.

Southern Sweet Cornbread

Servings: 6
Cooking Time: 17 Minutes
Ingredients:

- cooking spray
- ½ cup white cornmeal
- ½ cup flour
- 2 teaspoons baking powder
- ½ teaspoon salt
- 4 teaspoons sugar
- 1 egg
- 2 tablespoons oil
- ½ cup milk

Directions:

1. Preheat air fryer to 360°F.
2. Spray air fryer baking pan with nonstick cooking spray.
3. In a medium bowl, stir together the cornmeal, flour, baking powder, salt, and sugar.
4. In a small bowl, beat together the egg, oil, and milk. Stir into dry ingredients until well combined.
5. Pour batter into prepared baking pan.
6. Cook at 360°F for 17 minutes or until toothpick inserted in center comes out clean or with crumbs clinging.

Oat Bran Muffins

Servings: 8
Cooking Time: 12 Minutes
Ingredients:

- ⅔ cup oat bran
- ½ cup flour
- ¼ cup brown sugar
- 1 teaspoon baking powder
- ½ teaspoon baking soda
- ⅛ teaspoon salt
- ½ cup buttermilk
- 1 egg
- 2 tablespoons canola oil
- ½ cup chopped dates, raisins, or dried cranberries
- 24 paper muffin cups
- cooking spray

Directions:

1. Preheat air fryer to 330°F.
2. In a large bowl, combine the oat bran, flour, brown sugar, baking powder, baking soda, and salt.
3. In a small bowl, beat together the buttermilk, egg, and oil.
4. Pour buttermilk mixture into bowl with dry ingredients and stir just until moistened. Do not beat.
5. Gently stir in dried fruit.
6. Use triple baking cups to help muffins hold shape during baking. Spray them with cooking spray, place 4 sets of cups in air fryer basket at a time, and fill each one ¾ full of batter.
7. Cook for 12minutes, until top springs back when lightly touched and toothpick inserted in center comes out clean.
8. Repeat for remaining muffins.

Lemon-blueberry Morning Bread

Servings:2
Cooking Time: 15 Minutes
Ingredients:

- ½ cup flour
- ¼ cup powdered sugar
- ½ tsp baking powder
- ⅛ tsp salt
- 2 tbsp butter, melted
- 1 egg
- ½ tsp gelatin
- ½ tsp vanilla extract
- 1 tsp lemon zest
- ½ cup blueberries

Directions:

1. Preheat air fryer to 300ºF. Mix the flour, sugar, baking powder, and salt in a bowl. In another bowl, whisk the butter, egg, gelatin, lemon zest, vanilla extract, and blueberries. Add egg mixture to flour mixture and stir until smooth. Spoon mixture into a pizza pan. Place pan in the frying basket and Bake for 10 minutes. Let sit for 5 minutes before slicing. Serve immediately.

Peach Fritters

Servings: 8
Cooking Time: 6 Minutes
Ingredients:

- 1½ cups bread flour
- 1 teaspoon active dry yeast
- ¼ cup sugar
- ¼ teaspoon salt
- ½ cup warm milk
- ½ teaspoon vanilla extract
- 2 egg yolks
- 2 tablespoons melted butter
- 2 cups small diced peaches (fresh or frozen)
- 1 tablespoon butter
- 1 teaspoon ground cinnamon
- 1 to 2 tablespoons sugar
- Glaze
- ¾ cup powdered sugar
- 4 teaspoons milk

Directions:

1. Combine the flour, yeast, sugar and salt in a bowl. Add the milk, vanilla, egg yolks and melted butter and combine until the dough starts to come together. Transfer the dough to a floured surface and knead it by hand for 2 minutes. Shape the dough into a ball, place it in a large oiled bowl, cover with a clean kitchen towel and let the dough rise in a warm place for 1 to 1½ hours, or until the dough has doubled in size.

2. While the dough is rising, melt one tablespoon of butter in a medium saucepan on the stovetop. Add the diced peaches, cinnamon and sugar to taste. Cook the peaches for about 5 minutes, or until they soften. Set the peaches aside to cool.

3. When the dough has risen, transfer it to a floured surface and shape it into a 12-inch circle. Spread the peaches over half of the circle and fold the other half of the dough over the top. With a knife or a board scraper, score the dough by making slits in the dough in a diamond shape. Push the knife straight down into the dough and peaches, rather than slicing through. You should cut through the top layer of dough, but not the bottom. Roll the dough up into a log from one short end to the other. It should be roughly 8 inches long. Some of the peaches will be sticking out of the dough – don't worry, these are supposed to be a little random. Cut the log into 8 equal slices. Place the dough disks on a floured cookie sheet, cover with a clean kitchen towel and let rise in a warm place for 30 minutes.

4. Preheat the air fryer to 370°F.

5. Air-fry 2 or 3 fritters at a time at 370°F, for 3 minutes. Flip them over and continue to air-fry for another 2 to 3 minutes, until they are golden brown.

6. Combine the powdered sugar and milk together in a small bowl. Whisk vigorously until smooth. Allow the fritters to cool for at least 10 minutes and then brush the glaze over both the bottom and top of each one. Serve warm or at room temperature.

Appetizers And Snacks
Cheesy Green Dip

Servings: 6
Cooking Time: 30 Minutes
Ingredients:

- ½ cup canned artichoke hearts, chopped
- ½ cup cream cheese, softened
- 2 tbsp grated Romano cheese
- ¼ cup grated mozzarella
- ½ cup spinach, chopped
- ½ cup milk
- Salt and pepper to taste

Directions:
1. Preheat air fryer to 350°F. Whisk the milk, cream cheese, Romano cheese, spinach, artichoke hearts, salt, and pepper in a mixing bowl. Pour the mixture into a greased baking pan, and sprinkle the grated mozzarella cheese over the top. Bake in the air fryer for 20 minutes. Serve.

Hawaiian Ahi Tuna Bowls

Servings: 4
Cooking Time: 20 Minutes
Ingredients:

- 8 oz sushi-grade tuna steaks, cubed
- ½ peeled cucumber, diced
- 12 wonton wrappers
- ¾ cup dried beans
- 2 tbsp soy sauce
- 1 tsp toasted sesame oil
- ½ tsp Sriracha sauce
- 1 chili, minced
- 2 oz avocado, cubed
- ¼ cup sliced scallions
- 1 tbsp toasted sesame seeds

Directions:
1. Make wonton bowls by placing each wonton wrapper in a foil-lined baking cup. Press gently in the middle and against the sides. Use a light coating of cooking spray. Spoon a heaping tbsp of dried beans into the wonton cup.
2. Preheat air fryer to 280°F. Place the cups in a single layer on the frying basket. Bake until brown and crispy, 9-11 minutes. Using tongs, carefully remove the cups and allow them to cool slightly. Remove the beans and place the cups to the side. In a bowl, whisk together the chili, soy sauce, sesame oil, and sriracha. Toss in tuna, cucumber, avocado, and scallions. Place 2 heaping tbsp of the tuna mixture into each wonton cup. Top with sesame seeds and serve immediately.

Roasted Red Pepper Dip

Servings: 2
Cooking Time: 15 Minutes
Ingredients:

- 2 Medium-size red bell pepper(s)
- 1¾ cups (one 15-ounce can) Canned white beans, drained and rinsed
- 1 tablespoon Fresh oregano leaves, packed
- 3 tablespoons Olive oil
- 1 tablespoon Lemon juice
- ½ teaspoon Table salt
- ½ teaspoon Ground black pepper

Directions:

1. Preheat the air fryer to 400°F.
2. Set the pepper(s) in the basket and air-fry undisturbed for 15 minutes, until blistered and even blackened.
3. Use kitchen tongs to transfer the pepper(s) to a zip-closed plastic bag or small bowl. Seal the bag or cover the bowl with plastic wrap. Set aside for 20 minutes.
4. Peel each pepper, then stem it, cut it in half, and remove all its seeds and their white membranes.
5. Set the pieces of the pepper in a food processor. Add the beans, oregano, olive oil, lemon juice, salt, and pepper. Cover and process until smooth, stopping the machine at least once to scrape down the inside of the canister. Scrape the dip into a bowl and serve warm, or cover and refrigerate for up to 3 days (although the dip tastes best if it's allowed to come back to room temperature).

Asian-style Shrimp Toast

Servings: 4
Cooking Time: 25 Minutes
Ingredients:

- 8 large raw shrimp, chopped
- 1 egg white
- 2 garlic cloves, minced
- 1 red chili, minced
- 1 celery stalk, minced
- 2 tbsp cornstarch
- ¼ tsp Chinese five-spice
- 3 firm bread slices

Directions:

1. Preheat air fryer to 350°F. Add the shrimp, egg white, garlic, red chili, celery, corn starch, and five-spice powder in a bowl and combine. Place 1/3 of the shrimp mix on a slice of bread, smearing it to the edges, then slice the bread into 4 strips. Lay the strips in the frying basket in a single layer and Air Fry for 3-6 minutes until golden and crispy. Repeat until all strips are cooked. Serve hot.

Cauliflower-crust Pizza

Servings: 3
Cooking Time: 14 Minutes

Ingredients:

- 1 pound 2 ounces Riced cauliflower
- 1 plus 1 large egg yolk Large egg(s)
- 3 tablespoons (a little more than ½ ounce) Finely grated Parmesan cheese
- 1½ tablespoons Potato starch
- ¾ teaspoon Dried oregano
- ¾ teaspoon Table salt
- Vegetable oil spray
- 3 tablespoons Purchased pizza sauce
- 6 tablespoons (about 1½ ounces) Shredded semi-firm mozzarella

Directions:

1. Pour the riced cauliflower into a medium microwave-safe bowl. Microwave on high for 4 minutes. Stir well, then cool for 15 minutes.
2. Preheat the air fryer to 400°F.
3. Pour the riced cauliflower into a clean kitchen towel or a large piece of cheesecloth. Gather the towel or cheesecloth together. Working over the sink, squeeze the moisture out of the cauliflower, getting out as much of the liquid as you can.
4. Pour the squeezed cauliflower back into that same medium bowl and stir in the egg, egg yolk (if using), cheese, potato starch, oregano, and salt to form a loose, uniform "dough."
5. Cut a piece of aluminum foil or parchment paper into a 6-inch circle for a small pizza, a 7-inch circle for a medium one, or an 8-inch circle for a large one. Coat the circle with vegetable oil spray, then place it in the air-fryer basket. Using a small offset spatula or the back of a flatware tablespoon, spread and smooth the cauliflower mixture onto the circle right to the edges. Air-fry undisturbed for 10 minutes.
6. Remove the basket from the air fryer. Reduce the machine's temperature to 350°F .
7. Using a large nonstick safe spatula, flip over the cauliflower circle along with its foil or parchment paper right in the basket. Peel off and discard the foil or parchment paper. Spread the pizza sauce evenly over the crust and sprinkle with the cheese.
8. Air-fry undisturbed for 4 minutes, or until the cheese has melted and begun to bubble. Remove the basket from the machine and cool for 5 minutes. Use the same spatula to transfer the pizza to a wire rack to cool for 5 minutes more before cutting the pie into wedges to serve.

22

Honey-lemon Chicken Wings

Servings: 4
Cooking Time: 30 Minutes
Ingredients:

- 8 chicken wings
- Salt and pepper to taste
- 3 tbsp honey
- 1 tbsp lemon juice
- 1 tbsp chicken stock
- 2 cloves garlic, minced
- 2 thinly sliced green onions
- ¾ cup barbecue sauce
- 1 tbsp sesame seeds

Directions:

1. Preheat air fryer to 390°F. Season the wings with salt and pepper and place them in the frying basket. Air Fry for 20 minutes. Shake the basket a couple of times during cooking. In a bowl, mix the honey, lemon juice, chicken stock, and garlic. Take the wings out of the fryer and place them in a baking pan. Add the sauce and toss, coating completely. Put the pan in the air fryer and Air Fry for 4-5 minutes until golden and cooked through, with no pink showing. Top with green onions and sesame seeds, then serve with BBQ sauce.

Eggs In Avocado Halves

Servings: 3
Cooking Time: 23 Minutes
Ingredients:

- 3 Hass avocados, halved and pitted but not peeled
- 6 Medium eggs
- Vegetable oil spray
- 3 tablespoons Heavy or light cream (not fat-free cream)
- To taste Table salt
- To taste Ground black pepper

Directions:

1. Preheat the air fryer to 350°F .
2. Slice a small amount off the (skin) side of each avocado half so it can sit stable, without rocking. Lightly coat the skin of the avocado half (the side that will now sit stable) with vegetable oil spray.
3. Arrange the avocado halves open side up on a cutting board, then crack an egg into the indentation in each where the pit had been. If any white overflows the avocado half, wipe that bit of white off the cut edge of the avocado before proceeding.
4. Remove the basket (or its attachment) from the machine and set the filled avocado halves in it in one layer. Return it to the machine without pushing it in. Drizzle each avocado half with about 1½ teaspoons cream, a little salt, and a little ground black pepper.
5. Air-fry undisturbed for 10 minutes for a soft-set yolk, or air-fry for 13 minutes for more-set eggs.
6. Use a nonstick-safe spatula and a flatware fork for balance to transfer the avocado halves to serving plates. Cool a minute or two before serving.

Shrimp Toasts

Servings: 4
Cooking Time: 8 Minutes
Ingredients:

- ½ pound raw shrimp, peeled and de-veined
- 1 egg (or 2 egg whites)
- 2 scallions, plus more for garnish
- 2 teaspoons grated fresh ginger
- 1 teaspoon soy sauce
- ½ teaspoon toasted sesame oil
- 2 tablespoons chopped fresh cilantro or parsley
- 1 to 2 teaspoons sriracha sauce
- 6 slices thinly-sliced white sandwich bread (Pepperidge Farm®)
- ½ cup sesame seeds
- Thai chili sauce

Directions:

1. Combine the shrimp, egg, scallions, fresh ginger, soy sauce, sesame oil, cilantro (or parsley) and sriracha sauce in a food processor and process into a chunky paste, scraping down the sides of the food processor bowl as necessary.
2. Cut the crusts off the sandwich bread and generously spread the shrimp paste onto each slice of bread. Place the sesame seeds on a plate and invert each shrimp toast into the sesame seeds to coat, pressing down gently. Cut each slice of bread into 4 triangles.
3. Preheat the air fryer to 400°F.
4. Transfer one layer of shrimp toast triangles to the air fryer and air-fry at 400°F for 8 minutes, or until the sesame seeds are toasted on top.
5. Serve warm with a little Thai chili sauce and some sliced scallions as garnish.

Artichoke-spinach Dip

Servings: 4
Cooking Time: 25 Minutes
Ingredients:

- 4 oz canned artichoke hearts, chopped
- ½ cup Greek yogurt
- ¼ cup cream cheese
- ½ cup spinach, chopped
- ½ red bell pepper, chopped
- 1 garlic clove, minced
- ½ tsp dried oregano
- 3 tsp grated Parmesan cheese

Directions:

1. Preheat air fryer to 340°F. Mix the yogurt and cream cheese. Add the artichoke, spinach, red bell pepper, garlic, and oregano, then put the mix in a pan and scatter Parmesan cheese on top. Put the pan in the frying basket and Bake for 9-14 minutes. The dip should be bubble and brown. Serve hot.

Spanakopita Spinach, Feta And Pine Nut Phyllo Bites

Servings: 8
Cooking Time: 10 Minutes

Ingredients:

- ½ (10-ounce) package frozen spinach, thawed and squeezed dry (about 1 cup)
- ¾ cup crumbled feta cheese
- ¼ cup grated Parmesan cheese
- ¼ cup pine nuts, toasted
- ⅛ teaspoon ground nutmeg
- 1 egg, lightly beaten
- ½ teaspoon salt
- freshly ground black pepper
- 6 sheets phyllo dough
- ½ cup butter, melted

Directions:

1. Combine the spinach, cheeses, pine nuts, nutmeg and egg in a bowl. Season with salt and freshly ground black pepper.
2. While building the phyllo triangles, always keep the dough sheets you are not working with covered with plastic wrap and a damp clean kitchen towel. Remove one sheet of the phyllo and place it on a flat surface. Brush the phyllo sheet with melted butter and then layer another sheet of phyllo on top. Brush the second sheet of phyllo with butter. Cut the layered phyllo sheets into 6 strips, about 2½- to 3-inches wide.
3. Place a heaping tablespoon of the spinach filling at the end of each strip of dough. Fold the bottom right corner of the strip over the filling towards the left edge of the strip to make a triangle. Continue to fold the phyllo dough around the spinach as you would fold a flag, making triangle after triangle. Brush the outside of the phyllo triangle with more melted butter and set it aside until you've finished the 6 strips of dough, making 6 triangles.
4. Preheat the air fryer to 350°F.
5. Transfer the first six phyllo triangles to the air fryer basket and air-fry for 5 minutes. Turn the triangles over and air-fry for another 5 minutes.
6. While the first batch of triangles is air-frying, build another set of triangles and air-fry in the same manner. You should do three batches total. These can be warmed in the air fryer for a minute or two just before serving if you like.

Barbecue Chicken Nachos

Servings: 3
Cooking Time: 5 Minutes
Ingredients:

- 3 heaping cups (a little more than 3 ounces) Corn tortilla chips (gluten-free, if a concern)
- ¾ cup Shredded deboned and skinned rotisserie chicken meat (gluten-free, if a concern)
- 3 tablespoons Canned black beans, drained and rinsed
- 9 rings Pickled jalapeño slices
- 4 Small pickled cocktail onions, halved
- 3 tablespoons Barbecue sauce (any sort)
- ¾ cup (about 3 ounces) Shredded Cheddar cheese

Directions:

1. Preheat the air fryer to 400°F.
2. Cut a circle of parchment paper to line a 6-inch round cake pan for a small air fryer, a 7-inch round cake pan for a medium air fryer, or an 8-inch round cake pan for a large machine.
3. Fill the pan with an even layer of about two-thirds of the chips. Sprinkle the chicken evenly over the chips. Set the pan in the basket and air-fry undisturbed for 2 minutes.
4. Remove the basket from the machine. Scatter the beans, jalapeño rings, and pickled onion halves over the chicken. Drizzle the barbecue sauce over everything, then sprinkle the cheese on top.
5. Return the basket to the machine and air-fry undisturbed for 3 minutes, or until the cheese has melted and is bubbly. Remove the pan from the machine and cool for a couple of minutes before serving.

Fiery Cheese Sticks

Servings: 4
Cooking Time: 20 Minutes + Freezing Time
Ingredients:

- 1 egg, beaten
- ½ cup dried bread crumbs
- ¼ cup ground peanuts
- 1 tbsp chili powder
- ¼ tsp ground coriander
- ¼ tsp red pepper flakes
- ⅛ tsp cayenne pepper
- 8 mozzarella cheese sticks

Directions:

1. Preheat the air fryer to 375°F. Beat the egg in a bowl, and on a plate, combine the breadcrumbs, peanuts, coriander, chili powder, pepper flakes, and cayenne. Dip each piece of string cheese in the egg, then in the breadcrumb mix. After lining a baking sheet with parchment paper, put the sticks on it and freeze them for 30 minutes. Get the sticks out of the freezer and set in the frying basket in a single layer. Spritz them with cooking oil. Air Fry for 7-9 minutes until the exterior is golden and the interior is hot and melted. Serve hot with marinara or ranch sauce.

Easy Crab Cakes

Servings: 4
Cooking Time: 20 Minutes
Ingredients:

- 1 cup lump crab meat
- 2 green onions, minced
- 3 garlic cloves, minced
- ½ lime, juiced
- 2 tbsp mayonnaise
- 2 eggs, beaten
- 1 tsp fresh grated ginger
- ½ tsp allspice
- ½ cup breadcrumbs
- 2 tsp oyster sauce
- 2 tsp spicy mustard
- Pinch of black pepper

Directions:

1. Preheat air fryer to 350°F. Place the crab meat, lime juice, mayonnaise, onions, garlic, ginger, oyster sauce, mustard, allspice, and black pepper in a large mixing bowl. Stir thoroughly until all the ingredients are evenly combined.

2. Form the mixture into patties. Dip the patties into the beaten eggs, and then roll in the breadcrumbs, coating thoroughly on all sides. Place the coated cakes in the lined frying basket and Air Fry for 5 minutes. Flip the cakes over and cook for another 5 minutes until golden brown and crispy on the outside and tantalizingly juicy on the inside. Serve hot.

Chicken Shawarma Bites

Servings: 6
Cooking Time: 22 Minutes
Ingredients:

- 1½ pounds Boneless skinless chicken thighs, trimmed of any fat and cut into 1-inch pieces
- 1½ tablespoons Olive oil
- Up to 1½ tablespoons Minced garlic
- ½ teaspoon Table salt
- ¼ teaspoon Ground cardamom
- ¼ teaspoon Ground cinnamon
- ¼ teaspoon Ground cumin
- ¼ teaspoon Mild paprika
- Up to a ¼ teaspoon Grated nutmeg
- ¼ teaspoon Ground black pepper

Directions:

1. Preheat the air fryer to 400°F.

2. Mix all the ingredients in a large bowl until the chicken is thoroughly and evenly coated in the oil and spices.

3. When the machine is at temperature, scrape the coated chicken pieces into the basket and spread them out into one layer as much as you can. Air-fry for 22 minutes, shaking the basket at least three times during cooking to rearrange the pieces, until well browned and crisp.

4. Pour the chicken pieces onto a wire rack. Cool for 5 minutes before serving.

Spicy Sweet Potato Tater-tots

Servings: 6
Cooking Time: 10 Minutes
Ingredients:

- 6 cups filtered water
- 2 medium sweet potatoes, peeled and cut in half
- 1 teaspoon garlic powder
- ½ teaspoon black pepper, divided
- ½ teaspoon salt, divided
- 1 cup panko breadcrumbs
- 1 teaspoon blackened seasoning

Directions:

1. In a large stovetop pot, bring the water to a boil. Add the sweet potatoes and let boil about 10 minutes, until a metal fork prong can be inserted but the potatoes still have a slight give (not completely mashed).
2. Carefully remove the potatoes from the pot and let cool.
3. When you're able to touch them, grate the potatoes into a large bowl. Mix the garlic powder, ¼ teaspoon of the black pepper, and ¼ teaspoon of the salt into the potatoes. Place the mixture in the refrigerator and let set at least 45 minutes (if you're leaving them longer than 45 minutes, cover the bowl).
4. Before assembling, mix the breadcrumbs and blackened seasoning in a small bowl.
5. Remove the sweet potatoes from the refrigerator and preheat the air fryer to 400°F.
6. Assemble the tater-tots by using a teaspoon to portion batter evenly and form into a tater-tot shape. Roll each tater-tot in the breadcrumb mixture. Then carefully place the tater-tots in the air fryer basket. Be sure that you've liberally sprayed the air fryer basket with an olive oil mist. Repeat until tater-tots fill the basket without touching one another. You'll need to do multiple batches, depending on the size of your air fryer.
7. Cook the tater-tots for 3 to 6 minutes, flip, and cook another 3 to 6 minutes.
8. Remove from the air fryer carefully and keep warm until ready to serve.

Curly Kale Chips With Greek Sauce

Servings: 4
Cooking Time: 15 Minutes
Ingredients:

- 1 cup Greek yogurt
- 3 tbsp lemon juice
- ½ tsp mustard powder
- ½ tsp dried dill
- 1 tbsp ground walnuts
- 1 bunch curly kale
- 2 tbsp olive oil
- Salt and pepper to taste

Directions:

1. Preheat air fryer to 390°F. Mix together yogurt, lemon juice, mustard powder, ground walnuts, and dill until well blended. Set aside. Cut off the stems and ribs from the kale, then cut the leaves into 3-inch pieces.
2. In a bowl, toss the kale with olive oil, salt and pepper. Arrange the kale in the fryer and Air Fry for 2-3 minutes. Shake the basket, then cook for another 2-3 minutes or until the kale is crisp. Serve the chips with Greek sauce.

Asian Rice Logs

Servings: 8
Cooking Time: 5 Minutes
Ingredients:

- 1½ cups cooked jasmine or sushi rice
- ¼ teaspoon salt
- 2 teaspoons five-spice powder
- 2 teaspoons diced shallots
- 1 tablespoon tamari sauce
- 1 egg, beaten
- 1 teaspoon sesame oil
- 2 teaspoons water
- ⅓ cup plain breadcrumbs
- ¾ cup panko breadcrumbs
- 2 tablespoons sesame seeds
- Orange Marmalade Dipping Sauce
- ½ cup all-natural orange marmalade
- 1 tablespoon soy sauce

Directions:
1. Make the rice according to package instructions. While the rice is cooking, make the dipping sauce by combining the marmalade and soy sauce and set aside.
2. Stir together the cooked rice, salt, five-spice powder, shallots, and tamari sauce.
3. Divide rice into 8 equal pieces. With slightly damp hands, mold each piece into a log shape. Chill in freezer for 10 to 15minutes.
4. Mix the egg, sesame oil, and water together in a shallow bowl.
5. Place the plain breadcrumbs on a sheet of wax paper.
6. Mix the panko breadcrumbs with the sesame seeds and place on another sheet of wax paper.
7. Roll the rice logs in plain breadcrumbs, then dip in egg wash, and then dip in the panko and sesame seeds.
8. Cook the logs at 390°F for approximately 5minutes, until golden brown.
9. Cool slightly before serving with Orange Marmalade Dipping Sauce.

Bacon & Blue Cheese Tartlets

Servings: 6
Cooking Time: 30 Minutes
Ingredients:

- 6 bacon slices
- 16 phyllo tartlet shells
- ½ cup diced blue cheese
- 3 tbsp apple jelly

Directions:
1. Preheat the air fryer to 400°F. Put the bacon in a single layer in the frying basket and Air Fry for 14 minutes, turning once halfway through. Remove and drain on paper towels, then crumble when cool. Wipe the fryer clean. Fill the tartlet shells with bacon and the blue cheese cubes and add a dab of apple jelly on top of the filling. Lower the temperature to 350°F, then put the shells in the frying basket. Air Fry until the cheese melts and the shells brown, about 5-6 minutes. Remove and serve.

Crunchy Pickle Chips

Servings: 4
Cooking Time: 20 Minutes
Ingredients:

- 1 lb dill pickles, sliced
- 2 eggs
- 1/3 cup flour
- 1/3 cup bread crumbs
- 1 tsp Italian seasoning

Directions:
1. Preheat air fryer to 400°F. Set out three small bowls. In the first bowl, add flour. In the second bowl, beat eggs. In the third bowl, mix bread crumbs with Italian seasoning. Dip the pickle slices in the flour. Shake, then dredge in egg. Roll in bread crumbs and shake excess. Place the pickles in the greased frying basket and Air Fry for 6 minutes. Flip them halfway through cooking and fry for another 3 minutes until crispy. Serve warm.

Jalapeño Poppers

Servings: 18
Cooking Time: 5 Minutes
Ingredients:

- ½ pound jalapeño peppers
- ¼ cup cornstarch
- 1 egg
- 1 tablespoon lime juice
- ¼ cup plain breadcrumbs
- ¼ cup panko breadcrumbs
- ½ teaspoon salt
- oil for misting or cooking spray
- Filling
- 4 ounces cream cheese
- 1 teaspoon grated lime zest
- ¼ teaspoon chile powder
- ⅛ teaspoon garlic powder
- ¼ teaspoon salt

Directions:
1. Combine all filling ingredients in small bowl and mix well. Refrigerate while preparing peppers.
2. Cut jalapeños into ½-inch lengthwise slices. Use a small, sharp knife to remove seeds and veins.
3. a. For mild appetizers, discard seeds and veins.
4. b. For hot appetizers, finely chop seeds and veins. Stir a small amount into filling, taste, and continue adding a little at a time until filling is as hot as you like.
5. Stuff each pepper slice with filling.
6. Place cornstarch in a shallow dish.
7. In another shallow dish, beat together egg and lime juice.
8. Place breadcrumbs and salt in a third shallow dish and stir together.
9. Dip each pepper slice in cornstarch, shake off excess, then dip in egg mixture.
10. Roll in breadcrumbs, pressing to make coating stick.
11. Place pepper slices on a plate in single layer and freeze them for 30minutes.
12. Preheat air fryer to 390°F.
13. Spray frozen peppers with oil or cooking spray. Place in air fryer basket in a single layer and cook for 5minutes.

Beef , pork & Lamb Recipes
Egg Stuffed Pork Meatballs

Servings: 2
Cooking Time: 40 Minutes
Ingredients:

- 3 soft boiled eggs, peeled
- 8 oz ground pork
- 2 tsp dried tarragon
- ½ tsp hot paprika
- 2 tsp garlic powder
- Salt and pepper to taste

Directions:

1. Preheat air fryer to 350°F. Combine the pork, tarragon, hot paprika, garlic powder, salt, and pepper in a bowl and stir until all spices are evenly spread throughout the meat. Divide the meat mixture into three equal portions in the mixing bowl, and shape each into balls.

2. Flatten one of the meatballs on top to make a wide, flat meat circle. Place an egg in the middle. Use your hands to mold the mixture up and around to enclose the egg. Repeat with the remaining eggs. Place the stuffed balls in the air fryer. Air Fry for 18-20 minutes, shaking the basket once until the meat is crispy and golden brown. Serve.

Pizza Tortilla Rolls

Servings: 4
Cooking Time: 8 Minutes
Ingredients:

- 1 teaspoon butter
- ½ medium onion, slivered
- ½ red or green bell pepper, julienned
- 4 ounces fresh white mushrooms, chopped
- 8 flour tortillas (6- or 7-inch size)
- ½ cup pizza sauce
- 8 thin slices deli ham
- 24 pepperoni slices (about 1½ ounces)
- 1 cup shredded mozzarella cheese (about 4 ounces)
- oil for misting or cooking spray

Directions:

1. Place butter, onions, bell pepper, and mushrooms in air fryer baking pan. Cook at 390°F for 3minutes. Stir and cook 4 minutes longer until just crisp and tender. Remove pan and set aside.

2. To assemble rolls, spread about 2 teaspoons of pizza sauce on one half of each tortilla. Top with a slice of ham and 3 slices of pepperoni. Divide sautéed vegetables among tortillas and top with cheese.

3. Roll up tortillas, secure with toothpicks if needed, and spray with oil.

4. Place 4 rolls in air fryer basket and cook for 4minutes. Turn and cook 4 minutes, until heated through and lightly browned.

5. Repeat step 4 to cook remaining pizza rolls.

Perfect Pork Chops

Servings: 3
Cooking Time: 10 Minutes
Ingredients:

- ¾ teaspoon Mild paprika
- ¾ teaspoon Dried thyme
- ¾ teaspoon Onion powder
- ¼ teaspoon Garlic powder
- ¼ teaspoon Table salt
- ¼ teaspoon Ground black pepper
- 3 6-ounce boneless center-cut pork loin chops
- Vegetable oil spray

Directions:
1. Preheat the air fryer to 400°F.
2. Mix the paprika, thyme, onion powder, garlic powder, salt, and pepper in a small bowl until well combined. Massage this mixture into both sides of the chops. Generously coat both sides of the chops with vegetable oil spray.
3. When the machine is at temperature, set the chops in the basket with as much air space between them as possible. Air-fry undisturbed for 10 minutes, or until an instant-read meat thermometer inserted into the thickest part of a chop registers 145°F.
4. Use kitchen tongs to transfer the chops to a cutting board or serving plates. Cool for 5 minutes before serving.

Tandoori Lamb Samosas

Servings: 2
Cooking Time: 20 Minutes
Ingredients:

- 6 oz ground lamb, sautéed
- ¼ cup spinach, torn
- ½ onion, minced
- 1 tsp tandoori masala
- ½ tsp ginger-garlic paste
- ½ tsp red chili powder
- ½ tsp turmeric powder
- Salt and pepper to taste
- 3 puff dough sheets

Directions:
1. Preheat air fryer to 350°F. Put the ground lamb, tandoori masala, ginger garlic paste, red chili powder, turmeric powder, salt, and pepper in a bowl and stir to combine. Add in the spinach and onion and stir until the ingredients are evenly blended. Divide the mixture into three equal segments.
2. Lay the pastry dough sheets out on a lightly floured surface. Fill each sheet of dough with one of the three portions of lamb mix, then fold the pastry over into a triangle, sealing the edges with a bit of water. Transfer the samosas to the greased frying basket and Air Fry for 12 minutes, flipping once until the samosas are crispy and flaky. Remove and leave to cool for 5 minutes. Serve.

Extra Crispy Country-style Pork Riblets

Servings: 3
Cooking Time: 30 Minutes
Ingredients:

- ⅓ cup Tapioca flour
- 2½ tablespoons Chile powder
- ¾ teaspoon Table salt (optional)
- 1¼ pounds Boneless country-style pork ribs, cut into 1½-inch chunks
- Vegetable oil spray

Directions:

1. Preheat the air fryer to 375°F .
2. Mix the tapioca flour, chile powder, and salt (if using) in a large bowl until well combined. Add the country-style rib chunks and toss well to coat thoroughly.
3. When the machine is at temperature, gently shake off any excess tapioca coating from the chunks. Generously coat them on all sides with vegetable oil spray. Arrange the chunks in the basket in one (admittedly fairly tight) layer. The pieces may touch. Air-fry for 30 minutes, rearranging the pieces at the 10- and 20-minute marks to expose any touching bits, until very crisp and well browned.
4. Gently pour the contents of the basket onto a wire rack. Cool for 5 minutes before serving.

Crunchy Veal Cutlets

Servings: 2
Cooking Time: 5 Minutes
Ingredients:

- ½ cup All-purpose flour or tapioca flour
- 1 Large egg(s), well beaten
- ¾ cup Seasoned Italian-style dried bread crumbs (gluten-free, if a concern)
- 2 tablespoons Yellow cornmeal
- 4 Thinly pounded 2-ounce veal leg cutlets (less than ¼ inch thick)
- Olive oil spray

Directions:

1. Preheat the air fryer to 400°F.
2. Set up and fill three shallow soup plates or small pie plates on your counter: one for the flour; one for the egg(s); and one for the bread crumbs, whisked with the cornmeal until well combined.
3. Dredge a veal cutlet in the flour, coating it on both sides. Gently shake off any excess flour, then gently dip it in the beaten egg(s), coating both sides. Let the excess egg slip back into the rest. Dip the cutlet in the bread-crumb mixture, turning it several times and pressing gently to make an even coating on both sides. Coat it on both sides with olive oil spray, then set it aside and continue dredging and coating more cutlets.
4. When the machine is at temperature, set the cutlets in the basket so that they don't touch each other. Air-fry undisturbed for 5 minutes, or until crisp and brown. (If only some of the veal cutlets will fit in one layer for any selected batch—the sizes of air fryer baskets vary dramatically—work in batches as necessary.)
5. Use kitchen tongs to transfer the cutlets to a wire rack. Cool for only 1 to 2 minutes before serving.

Pesto-rubbed Veal Chops

Servings: 2
Cooking Time: 12-15 Minutes
Ingredients:

- ¼ cup Purchased pesto
- 2 10-ounce bone-in veal loin or rib chop(s)
- ½ teaspoon Ground black pepper

Directions:

1. Preheat the air fryer to 400°F.
2. Rub the pesto onto both sides of the veal chop(s). Sprinkle one side of the chop(s) with the ground black pepper. Set aside at room temperature as the machine comes up to temperature.
3. Set the chop(s) in the basket. If you're cooking more than one chop, leave as much air space between them as possible. Air-fry undisturbed for 12 minutes for medium-rare, or until an instant-read meat thermometer inserted into the center of a chop (without touching bone) registers 135°F (not USDA-approved). Or air-fry undisturbed for 15 minutes for medium-well, or until an instant-read meat thermometer registers 145°F (USDA-approved).
4. Use kitchen tongs to transfer the chops to a cutting board or a wire rack. Cool for 5 minutes before serving.

Beef & Barley Stuffed Bell Peppers

Servings: 4
Cooking Time: 30 Minutes
Ingredients:

- 1 cup pulled cooked roast beef
- 4 bell peppers, tops removed
- 1 onion, chopped
- ½ cup grated carrot
- 2 tsp olive oil
- 2 tomatoes, chopped
- 1 cup cooked barley
- 1 tsp dried marjoram

Directions:

1. Preheat air fryer to 400°F. Cut the tops of the bell peppers, then remove the stems. Put the onion, carrots, and olive oil in a baking pan and cook for 2-4 minutes. The veggies should be crispy but soft. Put the veggies in a bowl, toss in the tomatoes, barley, roast beef, and marjoram, and mix to combine. Spoon the veggie mix into the cleaned bell peppers and put them in the frying basket. Bake for 12-16 minutes or until the peppers are tender. Serve warm.

Mustard And Rosemary Pork Tenderloin With Fried Apples

Servings: 2
Cooking Time: 26 Minutes
Ingredients:

- 1 pork tenderloin (about 1-pound)
- 2 tablespoons coarse brown mustard
- salt and freshly ground black pepper
- 1½ teaspoons finely chopped fresh rosemary, plus sprigs for garnish
- 2 apples, cored and cut into 8 wedges
- 1 tablespoon butter, melted
- 1 teaspoon brown sugar

Directions:

1. Preheat the air fryer to 370°F.
2. Cut the pork tenderloin in half so that you have two pieces that fit into the air fryer basket. Brush the mustard onto both halves of the pork tenderloin and then season with salt, pepper and the fresh rosemary. Place the pork tenderloin halves into the air fryer basket and air-fry for 10 minutes. Turn the pork over and air-fry for an additional 8 minutes or until the internal temperature of the pork registers 155°F on an instant read thermometer. If your pork tenderloin is especially thick, you may need to add a minute or two, but it's better to check the pork and add time, than to overcook it.
3. Let the pork rest for 5 minutes. In the meantime, toss the apple wedges with the butter and brown sugar and air-fry at 400°F for 8 minutes, shaking the basket once or twice during the cooking process so the apples cook and brown evenly.
4. Slice the pork on the bias. Serve with the fried apples scattered over the top and a few sprigs of rosemary as garnish.

Italian Meatballs

Servings: 4
Cooking Time: 12 Minutes
Ingredients:

- 12 ounces lean ground beef
- 4 ounces Italian sausage, casing removed
- ½ cup breadcrumbs
- 1 cup grated Parmesan cheese
- 1 egg
- 2 tablespoons milk
- 2 teaspoons Italian seasoning
- ½ teaspoon onion powder
- ½ teaspoon garlic powder
- Pinch of red pepper flakes

Directions:

1. In a large bowl, place all the ingredients and mix well. Roll out 24 meatballs.
2. Preheat the air fryer to 360°F.
3. Place the meatballs in the air fryer basket and cook for 12 minutes, tossing every 4 minutes. Using a food thermometer, check to ensure the internal temperature of the meatballs is 165°F.

Tarragon Pork Tenderloin

Servings: 4
Cooking Time: 25 Minutes
Ingredients:
- ½ tsp dried tarragon
- 1 lb pork tenderloin, sliced
- Salt and pepper to taste
- 2 tbsp Dijon mustard
- 1 clove garlic, minced
- 1 cup bread crumbs
- 2 tbsp olive oil

Directions:
1. Preheat air fryer to 390°F. Using a rolling pin, pound the pork slices until they are about ¾ inch thick. Season both sides with salt and pepper. Coat the pork with mustard and season with garlic and tarragon. In a shallow bowl, mix bread crumbs and olive oil. Dredge the pork with the bread crumbs, pressing firmly, so that it adheres. Put the pork in the frying basket and Air Fry until the pork outside is brown and crisp, 12-14 minutes. Serve warm.

Chipotle Pork Meatballs

Servings:4
Cooking Time: 35 Minutes
Ingredients:
- 1 lb ground pork
- 1 egg
- ¼ cup chipotle sauce
- ¼ cup grated celery
- ¼ cup chopped parsley
- ¼ cup chopped cilantro
- ¼ cup flour
- ¼ tsp salt

Directions:
1. Preheat air fryer to 350°F. In a large bowl, combine the ground pork, egg, chipotle sauce, celery, parsley, cilantro, flour, and salt. Form mixture into 16 meatballs. Place the meatballs in the lightly greased frying basket and Air Fry for 8-10 minutes, flipping once. Serve immediately!

Wiener Schnitzel

Servings: 4
Cooking Time: 14 Minutes
Ingredients:

- 4 thin boneless pork loin chops
- 2 tablespoons lemon juice
- ½ cup flour
- 1 teaspoon salt
- ¼ teaspoon marjoram
- 1 cup plain breadcrumbs
- 2 eggs, beaten
- oil for misting or cooking spray

Directions:

1. Rub the lemon juice into all sides of pork chops.
2. Mix together the flour, salt, and marjoram.
3. Place flour mixture on a sheet of wax paper.
4. Place breadcrumbs on another sheet of wax paper.
5. Roll pork chops in flour, dip in beaten eggs, then roll in breadcrumbs. Mist all sides with oil or cooking spray.
6. Spray air fryer basket with nonstick cooking spray and place pork chops in basket.
7. Cook at 390°F for 7minutes. Turn, mist again, and cook for another 7 minutes, until well done. Serve with lemon wedges.

Mustard-crusted Rib-eye

Servings: 2
Cooking Time: 9 Minutes
Ingredients:

- Two 6-ounce rib-eye steaks, about 1-inch thick
- 1 teaspoon coarse salt
- ½ teaspoon coarse black pepper
- 2 tablespoons Dijon mustard

Directions:

1. Rub the steaks with the salt and pepper. Then spread the mustard on both sides of the steaks. Cover with foil and let the steaks sit at room temperature for 30 minutes.
2. Preheat the air fryer to 390°F.
3. Cook the steaks for 9 minutes. Check for an internal temperature of 140°F and immediately remove the steaks and let them rest for 5 minutes before slicing.

Pork Schnitzel With Dill Sauce

Servings: 4
Cooking Time: 4 Minutes
Ingredients:

- 6 boneless, center cut pork chops (about 1½ pounds)
- ½ cup flour
- 1½ teaspoons salt
- freshly ground black pepper
- 2 eggs
- ½ cup milk
- 1½ cups toasted fine breadcrumbs
- 1 teaspoon paprika

- 3 tablespoons butter, melted
- 2 tablespoons vegetable or olive oil
- lemon wedges
- Dill Sauce:
- 1 cup chicken stock
- 1½ tablespoons cornstarch
- ⅓ cup sour cream
- 1½ tablespoons chopped fresh dill
- salt and pepper

Directions:

1. Trim the excess fat from the pork chops and pound each chop with a meat mallet between two pieces of plastic wrap until they are ½-inch thick.

2. Set up a dredging station. Combine the flour, salt, and black pepper in a shallow dish. Whisk the eggs and milk together in a second shallow dish. Finally, combine the breadcrumbs and paprika in a third shallow dish.

3. Dip each flattened pork chop in the flour. Shake off the excess flour and dip each chop into the egg mixture. Finally dip them into the breadcrumbs and press the breadcrumbs onto the meat firmly. Place each finished chop on a baking sheet until they are all coated.

4. Preheat the air fryer to 400°F.

5. Combine the melted butter and the oil in a small bowl and lightly brush both sides of the coated pork chops. Do not brush the chops too heavily or the breading will not be as crispy.

6. Air-fry one schnitzel at a time for 4 minutes, turning it over halfway through the cooking time. Hold the cooked schnitzels warm on a baking pan in a 170°F oven while you finish air-frying the rest.

7. While the schnitzels are cooking, whisk the chicken stock and cornstarch together in a small saucepan over medium-high heat on the stovetop. Bring the mixture to a boil and simmer for 2 minutes. Remove the saucepan from heat and whisk in the sour cream. Add the chopped fresh dill and season with salt and pepper.

8. Transfer the pork schnitzel to a platter and serve with dill sauce and lemon wedges. For a traditional meal, serve this along side some egg noodles, spätzle or German potato salad.

Mongolian Beef

Servings: 4
Cooking Time: 15 Minutes

Ingredients:

- 1½ pounds flank steak, thinly sliced
- on the bias into ¼-inch strips
- Marinade
- 2 tablespoons soy sauce*
- 1 clove garlic, smashed
- big pinch crushed red pepper flakes
- Sauce
- 1 tablespoon vegetable oil
- 2 cloves garlic, minced
- 1 tablespoon finely grated fresh ginger
- 3 dried red chili peppers
- ¾ cup soy sauce*
- ¾ cup chicken stock
- 5 to 6 tablespoons brown sugar (depending on how sweet you want the sauce)
- ½ cup cornstarch, divided
- 1 bunch scallions, sliced into 2-inch pieces

Directions:

1. Marinate the beef in the soy sauce, garlic and red pepper flakes for one hour.
2. In the meantime, make the sauce. Preheat a small saucepan over medium heat on the stovetop. Add the oil, garlic, ginger and dried chili peppers and sauté for just a minute or two. Add the soy sauce, chicken stock and brown sugar and continue to simmer for a few minutes. Dissolve 3 tablespoons of cornstarch in 3 tablespoons of water and stir this into the saucepan. Stir the sauce over medium heat until it thickens. Set this aside.
3. Preheat the air fryer to 400°F.
4. Remove the beef from the marinade and transfer it to a zipper sealable plastic bag with the remaining cornstarch. Shake it around to completely coat the beef and transfer the coated strips of beef to a baking sheet or plate, shaking off any excess cornstarch. Spray the strips with vegetable oil on all sides and transfer them to the air fryer basket.
5. Air-fry at 400°F for 15 minutes, shaking the basket to toss and rotate the beef strips throughout the cooking process. Add the scallions for the last 4 minutes of the cooking. Transfer the hot beef strips and scallions to a bowl and toss with the sauce (warmed on the stovetop if necessary), coating all the beef strips with the sauce. Serve warm over white rice.

Herby Lamb Chops

Servings: 2
Cooking Time: 25 Minutes
Ingredients:

- 3 lamb chops
- 1 cup breadcrumbs
- 2 eggs, beaten
- Salt and pepper to taste
- ½ tbsp thyme
- ½ tbsp mint, chopped
- ½ tsp garlic powder
- ½ tsp ground rosemary
- ½ tsp cayenne powder
- ½ tsp ras el hanout

Directions:

1. Preheat air fryer to 320°F. Mix the breadcrumbs, thyme, mint, garlic, rosemary, cayenne, ras el hanout, salt, and pepper in a bowl. Dip the lamb chops in the beaten eggs, then coat with the crumb mixture. Air Fry for 14-16 minutes, turning once. Serve and enjoy!

Fusion Tender Flank Steak

Servings: 4
Cooking Time: 25 Minutes
Ingredients:

- 2 tbsp cilantro, chopped
- 2 tbsp chives, chopped
- ¼ tsp red pepper flakes
- 1 jalapeño pepper, minced
- 1 lime, juiced
- 3 tbsp olive oil
- Salt and pepper to taste
- 2 tbsp sesame oil
- 5 tbsp tamari sauce
- 3 tsp honey
- 1 tbsp grated fresh ginger
- 2 green onions, minced
- 2 garlic cloves, minced
- 1 ¼ pounds flank steak

Directions:

1. Combine the jalapeño pepper, cilantro, chives, lime juice, olive oil, salt, and pepper in a bowl. Set aside. Mix the sesame oil, tamari sauce, honey, ginger, green onions, garlic, and pepper flakes in another bowl. Stir until the honey is dissolved. Put the steak into the bowl and massage the marinade onto the meat. Marinate for 2 hours in the fridge. Preheat air fryer to 390 F.
2. Remove the steak from the marinade and place it in the greased frying basket. Air Fry for about 6 minutes, flip, and continue cooking for 6-8 more minutes. Allow to rest for a few minutes, slice thinly against the grain and top with the prepared dressing. Serve and enjoy!

Tuscan Veal Chops

Servings: 2
Cooking Time: 12-15 Minutes
Ingredients:

- 4 teaspoons Olive oil
- 2 teaspoons Finely minced garlic
- 2 teaspoons Finely minced fresh rosemary leaves
- 1 teaspoon Finely grated lemon zest
- 1 teaspoon Crushed fennel seeds
- 1 teaspoon Table salt
- Up to ¼ teaspoon Red pepper flakes
- 2 10-ounce bone-in veal loin or rib chop(s), about ½ inch thick

Directions:

1. Preheat the air fryer to 400°F.
2. Mix the oil, garlic, rosemary, lemon zest, fennel seeds, salt, and red pepper flakes in a small bowl. Rub this mixture onto both sides of the veal chop(s). Set aside at room temperature as the machine comes to temperature.
3. Set the chop(s) in the basket. If you're cooking more than one chop, leave as much air space between them as possible. Air-fry undisturbed for 12 minutes for medium-rare, or until an instant-read meat thermometer inserted into the center of a chop (without touching bone) registers 135°F (not USDA-approved). Or air-fry undisturbed for 15 minutes for medium-well, or until an instant-read meat thermometer registers 145°F (USDA-approved).
4. Use kitchen tongs to transfer the chops to a cutting board or a wire rack. Cool for 5 minutes before serving.

Kentucky-style Pork Tenderloin

Servings:2
Cooking Time: 30 Minutes
Ingredients:

- 1 lb pork tenderloin, halved crosswise
- 1 tbsp smoked paprika
- 2 tsp ground cumin
- 1 tsp garlic powder
- 1 tsp shallot powder
- ¼ tsp chili pepper
- Salt and pepper to taste
- 1 tsp Italian seasoning
- 2 tbsp butter, melted
- 1 tsp Worcestershire sauce

Directions:

1. Preheat air fryer to 350ºF. In a shallow bowl, combine all spices. Set aside. In another bowl, whisk butter and Worcestershire sauce and brush over pork tenderloin. Sprinkle with the seasoning mix. Place pork in the lightly greased frying basket and Air Fry for 16 minutes, flipping once. Let sit onto a cutting board for 5 minutes before slicing. Serve immediately.

Poultry Recipes
Poblano Bake

Servings: 4
Cooking Time: 11 Minutes Per Batch

Ingredients:

- 2 large poblano peppers (approx. 5½ inches long excluding stem)
- ¾ pound ground turkey, raw
- ¾ cup cooked brown rice
- 1 teaspoon chile powder
- ½ teaspoon ground cumin
- ½ teaspoon garlic powder
- 4 ounces sharp Cheddar cheese, grated
- 1 8-ounce jar salsa, warmed

Directions:

1. Slice each pepper in half lengthwise so that you have four wide, flat pepper halves.
2. Remove seeds and membrane and discard. Rinse inside and out.
3. In a large bowl, combine turkey, rice, chile powder, cumin, and garlic powder. Mix well.
4. Divide turkey filling into 4 portions and stuff one into each of the 4 pepper halves. Press lightly to pack down.
5. Place 2 pepper halves in air fryer basket and cook at 390°F for 10minutes or until turkey is well done.
6. Top each pepper half with ¼ of the grated cheese. Cook 1 more minute or just until cheese melts.
7. Repeat steps 5 and 6 to cook remaining pepper halves.
8. To serve, place each pepper half on a plate and top with ¼ cup warm salsa.

Crispy Chicken Tenders

Servings: 4
Cooking Time: 20 Minutes

Ingredients:

- 1 egg
- ¼ cup almond milk
- ¼ cup almond flour
- ¼ cup bread crumbs
- Salt and pepper to taste
- ½ tsp dried thyme
- ½ tsp dried sage
- ½ tsp garlic powder
- ½ tsp chili powder
- 1 lb chicken tenderloins
- 1 lemon, quartered

Directions:

1. Preheat air fryer to 360°F. Whisk together the egg and almond milk in a bowl until frothy. Mix the flour, bread crumbs, salt, pepper, thyme, sage, chili powder and garlic powder in a separate bowl. Dip each chicken tenderloin into the egg mixture, then coat with the bread crumb mixture. Put the breaded chicken tenderloins into the frying basket in a single layer. Air Fry for 12 minutes, turning once. Serve with lemon slices.

Vip's Club Sandwiches

Servings: 4
Cooking Time: 50 Minutes
Ingredients:

- 1 cup buttermilk
- 1 egg
- 1 cup bread crumbs
- 1 tsp garlic powder
- Salt and pepper to taste
- 4 chicken cutlets
- 3 tbsp butter, melted
- 4 hamburger buns
- 4 tbsp mayonnaise
- 4 tsp yellow mustard
- 8 dill pickle chips
- 4 pieces iceberg lettuce
- ½ sliced avocado
- 4 slices cooked bacon
- 8 vine-ripe tomato slices
- 1 tsp chia seeds

Directions:

1. Preheat air fryer at 400°F. Beat the buttermilk and egg in a bowl. In another bowl, combine breadcrumbs, garlic powder, salt, and black pepper. Dip chicken cutlets in the egg mixture, then dredge them in the breadcrumbs mixture. Brush chicken cutlets lightly with melted butter on both sides, place them in the greased frying basket, and Air Fry for 18-20 minutes. Spread the mayonnaise on the top buns and mustard on the bottom buns. Add chicken onto bottom buns and top with pickles, lettuce, chia seeds, avocado, bacon, and tomato. Cover with the top buns. Serve and enjoy!

Mexican Turkey Meatloaves

Servings: 4
Cooking Time: 30 Minutes
Ingredients:

- ¼ cup jarred chunky mild salsa
- 1 lb ground turkey
- 1/3 cup bread crumbs
- 1/3 cup canned black beans
- 1/3 cup frozen corn
- ¼ cup minced onion
- ¼ cup chopped scallions
- 2 tbsp chopped cilantro
- 1 egg, beaten
- 1 tbsp tomato puree
- 1 tsp salt
- ½ tsp ground cumin
- 1 tsp Mulato chile powder
- ½ tsp ground aniseed
- ¼ tsp ground cloves
- 2 tbsp ketchup
- 2 tbsp jarred mild salsa

Directions:

1. In a bowl, use your hands to mix the turkey, bread crumbs, beans, corn, salsa, onion, scallions, cilantro, egg, tomato puree, salt, chile powder, aniseed, cloves, and cumin. Shape into 4 patties about 1-inch in thickness.
2. Preheat air fryer to 350°F. Put the meatloaves in the greased frying basket and Bake for about 18-20 minutes, flipping once until cooked through. Stir together the ketchup and salsa in a small bowl. When all loaves are cooked, brush them with the glaze and return to the fryer to heat up for 2 minutes. Serve immediately.

Satay Chicken Skewers

Servings: 4
Cooking Time: 35 Minutes
Ingredients:

- 2 chicken breasts, cut into strips
- 1 ½ tbsp Thai red curry paste
- ¼ cup peanut butter
- 1 tbsp maple syrup
- 1 tbsp tamari
- 1 tbsp lime juice
- 2 tsp chopped onions
- ¼ tsp minced ginger
- 1 clove garlic, minced
- 1 cup coconut milk
- 1 tsp fish sauce
- 1 tbsp chopped cilantro

Directions:

1. Mix the peanut butter, maple syrup, tamari, lime juice, ¼ tsp of sriracha, onions, ginger, garlic, and 2 tbsp of water in a bowl. Reserve 1 tbsp of the sauce. Set aside. Combine the reserved peanut sauce, fish sauce, coconut milk, Thai red curry paste, cilantro and chicken strips in a bowl and let marinate in the fridge for 15 minutes.
2. Preheat air fryer at 350ºF. Thread chicken strips onto skewers and place them on a kebab rack. Place rack in the frying basket and Air Fry for 12 minutes. Serve with previously prepared peanut sauce on the side.

Italian-inspired Chicken Pizzadillas

Servings: 4
Cooking Time: 25 Minutes
Ingredients:

- 2 cups cooked boneless, skinless chicken, shredded
- 1 cup grated provolone cheese
- 8 basil and menta leaves, julienned
- ½ tsp salt
- 1 tsp garlic powder
- 3 tbsp butter, melted
- 8 flour tortillas
- 1 cup marinara sauce
- 1 cup grated cheddar cheese

Directions:

1. Preheat air fryer at 350ºF. Sprinkle chicken with salt and garlic powder. Brush on one side of a tortilla lightly with melted butter. Spread ¼ cup of marinara sauce, then top with ½ cup of chicken, ¼ cup of cheddar cheese, ¼ cup of provolone, and finally, ¼ of basil and menta leaves. Top with a second tortilla and lightly brush with butter on top. Repeat with the remaining ingredients. Place quesadillas, butter side down, in the frying basket and Bake for 3 minutes. Cut them into 6 sections and serve.

Enchilada Chicken Quesadillas

Servings: 4
Cooking Time: 35 Minutes
Ingredients:

- 2 cups cooked chicken breasts, shredded
- 1 can diced green chilies, including juice
- 2 cups grated Mexican cheese blend
- 3/4 cup sour cream
- 2 tsp chili powder
- 1 tsp cumin
- 1 tbsp chipotle sauce
- 1 tsp dried onion flakes
- ½ tsp salt
- 3 tbsp butter, melted
- 8 flour tortillas

Directions:

1. In a small bowl, whisk the sour cream, chipotle sauce and chili powder. Let chill in the fridge until ready to use.
2. Preheat air fryer at 350ºF. Mix the chicken, green chilies, cumin, and salt in a bowl. Set aside. Brush on one side of a tortilla lightly with melted butter. Layer with ¼ cup of chicken, onion flakes and ¼ cup of Mexican cheese. Top with a second tortilla and lightly brush with butter on top. Repeat with the remaining ingredients. Place quesadillas, butter side down, in the frying basket and Bake for 3 minutes. Cut them into 6 sections and serve with cream sauce on the side.

Guajillo Chile Chicken Meatballs

Servings:4
Cooking Time: 30 Minutes
Ingredients:

- 1 lb ground chicken
- 1 large egg
- ½ cup bread crumbs
- 1 tbsp sour cream
- 2 tsp brown mustard
- 2 tbsp grated onion
- 2 tbsp tomato paste
- 1 tsp ground cumin
- 1 tsp guajillo chile powder
- 2 tbsp olive oil

Directions:

1. Preheat air fryer to 350ºF. Mix the ground chicken, egg, bread crumbs, sour cream, mustard, onion, tomato paste, cumin, and chili powder in a bowl. Form into 16 meatballs. Place the meatballs in the greased frying basket and Air Fry for 8-10 minutes, shaking once until browned and cooked through. Serve immediately.

Buffalo Egg Rolls

Servings: 8
Cooking Time: 9 Minutes Per Batch
Ingredients:

- 1 teaspoon water
- 1 tablespoon cornstarch
- 1 egg
- 2½ cups cooked chicken, diced or shredded (see opposite page)
- ⅓ cup chopped green onion
- ⅓ cup diced celery
- ⅓ cup buffalo wing sauce
- 8 egg roll wraps
- oil for misting or cooking spray
- Blue Cheese Dip
- 3 ounces cream cheese, softened
- ⅓ cup blue cheese, crumbled
- 1 teaspoon Worcestershire sauce
- ¼ teaspoon garlic powder
- ¼ cup buttermilk (or sour cream)

Directions:

1. Mix water and cornstarch in a small bowl until dissolved. Add egg, beat well, and set aside.
2. In a medium size bowl, mix together chicken, green onion, celery, and buffalo wing sauce.
3. Divide chicken mixture evenly among 8 egg roll wraps, spooning ½ inch from one edge.
4. Moisten all edges of each wrap with beaten egg wash.
5. Fold the short ends over filling, then roll up tightly and press to seal edges.
6. Brush outside of wraps with egg wash, then spritz with oil or cooking spray.
7. Place 4 egg rolls in air fryer basket.
8. Cook at 390°F for 9minutes or until outside is brown and crispy.
9. While the rolls are cooking, prepare the Blue Cheese Dip. With a fork, mash together cream cheese and blue cheese.
10. Stir in remaining ingredients.
11. Dip should be just thick enough to slightly cling to egg rolls. If too thick, stir in buttermilk or milk 1 tablespoon at a time until you reach the desired consistency.
12. Cook remaining 4 egg rolls as in steps 7 and 8.
13. Serve while hot with Blue Cheese Dip, more buffalo wing sauce, or both.

Teriyaki Chicken Legs

Servings: 2
Cooking Time: 20 Minutes
Ingredients:

- 4 tablespoons teriyaki sauce
- 1 tablespoon orange juice
- 1 teaspoon smoked paprika
- 4 chicken legs
- cooking spray

Directions:

1. Mix together the teriyaki sauce, orange juice, and smoked paprika. Brush on all sides of chicken legs.
2. Spray air fryer basket with nonstick cooking spray and place chicken in basket.
3. Cook at 360°F for 6minutes. Turn and baste with sauce. Cook for 6 moreminutes, turn and baste. Cook for 8 minutes more, until juices run clear when chicken is pierced with a fork.

Nacho Chicken Fries

Servings: 4
Cooking Time: 7 Minutes
Ingredients:

- 1 pound chicken tenders
- salt
- ¼ cup flour
- 2 eggs
- ¾ cup panko breadcrumbs
- ¾ cup crushed organic nacho cheese tortilla chips

- oil for misting or cooking spray
- Seasoning Mix
- 1 tablespoon chili powder
- 1 teaspoon ground cumin
- ½ teaspoon garlic powder
- ½ teaspoon onion powder

Directions:
1. Stir together all seasonings in a small cup and set aside.
2. Cut chicken tenders in half crosswise, then cut into strips no wider than about ½ inch.
3. Preheat air fryer to 390°F.
4. Salt chicken to taste. Place strips in large bowl and sprinkle with 1 tablespoon of the seasoning mix. Stir well to distribute seasonings.
5. Add flour to chicken and stir well to coat all sides.
6. Beat eggs together in a shallow dish.
7. In a second shallow dish, combine the panko, crushed chips, and the remaining 2 teaspoons of seasoning mix.
8. Dip chicken strips in eggs, then roll in crumbs. Mist with oil or cooking spray.
9. Chicken strips will cook best if done in two batches. They can be crowded and overlapping a little but not stacked in double or triple layers.
10. Cook for 4minutes. Shake basket, mist with oil, and cook 3 moreminutes, until chicken juices run clear and outside is crispy.
11. Repeat step 10 to cook remaining chicken fries.

Moroccan-style Chicken Strips

Servings: 4
Cooking Time: 30 Minutes
Ingredients:

- 4 chicken breasts, cut into strips
- 2 tsp olive oil
- 2 tbsp cornstarch
- 3 garlic cloves, minced
- ½ cup chicken broth

- ¼ cup lemon juice
- 1 tbsp honey
- ½ tsp ras el hanout
- 1 cup cooked couscous

Directions:
1. Preheat air fryer to 400°F. Mix the chicken and olive oil in a bowl, then add the cornstarch. Stir to coat. Add the garlic and transfer to a baking pan. Put the pan in the fryer. Bake for 10 minutes. Stir at least once during cooking.
2. When done, pour in the chicken broth, lemon juice, honey, and ras el hanout. Bake for an additional 6-9 minutes or until the sauce is thick and the chicken cooked through with no pink showing. Serve with couscous.

Fiesta Chicken Plate

Servings: 4
Cooking Time: 15 Minutes
Ingredients:

- 1 pound boneless, skinless chicken breasts (2 large breasts)
- 2 tablespoons lime juice
- 1 teaspoon cumin
- ½ teaspoon salt
- ½ cup grated Pepper Jack cheese
- 1 16-ounce can refried beans
- ½ cup salsa
- 2 cups shredded lettuce
- 1 medium tomato, chopped
- 2 avocados, peeled and sliced
- 1 small onion, sliced into thin rings
- sour cream
- tortilla chips (optional)

Directions:

1. Split each chicken breast in half lengthwise.
2. Mix lime juice, cumin, and salt together and brush on all surfaces of chicken breasts.
3. Place in air fryer basket and cook at 390°F for 15 minutes, until well done.
4. Divide the cheese evenly over chicken breasts and cook for an additional minute to melt cheese.
5. While chicken is cooking, heat refried beans on stovetop or in microwave.
6. When ready to serve, divide beans among 4 plates. Place chicken breasts on top of beans and spoon salsa over. Arrange the lettuce, tomatoes, and avocados artfully on each plate and scatter with the onion rings.
7. Pass sour cream at the table and serve with tortilla chips if desired.

Cal-mex Turkey Patties

Servings: 4
Cooking Time: 30 Minutes
Ingredients:

- 1/3 cup crushed corn tortilla chips
- 1/3 cup grated American cheese
- 1 egg, beaten
- ¼ cup salsa
- Salt and pepper to taste
- 1 lb ground turkey
- 1 tbsp olive oil
- 1 tsp chili powder

Directions:

1. Preheat air fryer to 330°F. Mix together egg, tortilla chips, salsa, cheese, salt, and pepper in a bowl. Using your hands, add the ground turkey and mix gently until just combined. Divide the meat into 4 equal portions and shape into patties about ½ inch thick. Brush the patties with olive oil and sprinkle with chili powder. Air Fry the patties for 14-16 minutes, flipping once until cooked through and golden. Serve and enjoy!

Chicken Cordon Bleu Patties

Servings: 4
Cooking Time: 30 Minutes
Ingredients:

- 1/3 cup grated Fontina cheese
- 3 tbsp milk
- 1/3 cup bread crumbs
- 1 egg, beaten
- ½ tsp dried parsley
- Salt and pepper to taste
- 1 ¼ lb ground chicken
- ¼ cup finely chopped ham

Directions:

1. Preheat air fryer to 350°F. Mix milk, breadcrumbs, egg, parsley, salt and pepper in a bowl. Using your hands, add the chicken and gently mix until just combined. Divide into 8 portions and shape into thin patties. Place on waxed paper. On 4 of the patties, top with ham and Fontina cheese, then place another patty on top of that. Gently pinch the edges together so that none of the ham or cheese is peeking out. Arrange the burgers in the greased frying basket and Air Fry until cooked through, for 14-16 minutes. Serve and enjoy!

Fiery Chicken Meatballs

Servings: 4
Cooking Time: 20 Minutes + Chilling Time
Ingredients:

- 2 jalapeños, seeded and diced
- 2 tbsp shredded Cheddar cheese
- 1 tsp Quick Pickled Jalapeños
- 2 tbsp white wine vinegar
- ½ tsp granulated sugar
- Salt and pepper to taste
- 1 tbsp ricotta cheese
- ¾ lb ground chicken
- ¼ tsp smoked paprika
- 1 tsp garlic powder
- 1 cup bread crumbs
- ¼ tsp salt

Directions:

1. Combine the jalapeños, white wine vinegar, sugar, black pepper, and salt in a bowl. Let sit the jalapeño mixture in the fridge for 15 minutes. In a bowl, combine ricotta cheese, cheddar cheese, and 1 tsp of the jalapeños. Form mixture into 8 balls. Mix the ground chicken, smoked paprika, garlic powder, and salt in a bowl. Form mixture into 8 meatballs. Form a hole in the chicken meatballs, press a cheese ball into the hole and form chicken around the cheese ball, sealing the cheese ball in meatballs.
2. Preheat air fryer at 350ºF. Mix the breadcrumbs and salt in a bowl. Roll stuffed meatballs in the mixture. Place the meatballs in the greased frying basket. Air Fry for 10 minutes, turning once. Serve immediately.

Jerk Chicken Drumsticks

Servings: 2
Cooking Time: 20 Minutes
Ingredients:

- 1 or 2 cloves garlic
- 1 inch of fresh ginger
- 2 serrano peppers, (with seeds if you like it spicy, seeds removed for less heat)
- 1 teaspoon ground allspice
- 1 teaspoon ground nutmeg
- 1 teaspoon chili powder
- ½ teaspoon dried thyme
- ½ teaspoon ground cinnamon
- ½ teaspoon paprika
- 1 tablespoon brown sugar
- 1 teaspoon soy sauce
- 2 tablespoons vegetable oil
- 6 skinless chicken drumsticks

Directions:

1. Combine all the ingredients except the chicken in a small chopper or blender and blend to a paste. Make slashes into the meat of the chicken drumsticks and rub the spice blend all over the chicken (a pair of plastic gloves makes this really easy). Transfer the rubbed chicken to a non-reactive covered container and let the chicken marinate for at least 30 minutes or overnight in the refrigerator.
2. Preheat the air fryer to 400°F.
3. Transfer the drumsticks to the air fryer basket. Air-fry for 10 minutes. Turn the drumsticks over and air-fry for another 10 minutes. Serve warm with some rice and vegetables or a green salad.

Chicken & Fruit Biryani

Servings: 4
Cooking Time: 30 Minutes
Ingredients:

- 3 chicken breasts, cubed
- 2 tsp olive oil
- 2 tbsp cornstarch
- 1 tbsp curry powder
- 1 apple, chopped
- ½ cup chicken broth
- 1/3 cup dried cranberries
- 1 cooked basmati rice

Directions:

1. Preheat air fryer to 380°F. Combine the chicken and olive oil, then add some corn starch and curry powder. Mix to coat, then add the apple and pour the mix in a baking pan. Put the pan in the air fryer and Bake for 8 minutes, stirring once. Add the chicken broth, cranberries, and 2 tbsp of water and continue baking for 10 minutes, letting the sauce thicken. The chicken should be lightly charred and cooked through. Serve warm with basmati rice.

Katsu Chicken Thighs

Servings: 4
Cooking Time: 35 Minutes
Ingredients:

- 1 ½ lb boneless, skinless chicken thighs
- 3 tbsp tamari sauce
- 3 tbsp lemon juice
- ½ tsp ground ginger
- Black pepper to taste
- 6 tbsp cornstarch
- 1 cup chicken stock
- 2 tbsp hoisin sauce
- 2 tbsp light brown sugar
- 2 tbsp sesame seeds

Directions:

1. Preheat the air fryer to 400°F. After cubing the chicken thighs, put them in a cake pan. Add a tbsp of tamari sauce, a tbsp of lemon juice, ginger, and black pepper. Mix and let marinate for 10 minutes. Remove the chicken and coat it in 4 tbsp of cornstarch; set aside. Add the rest of the marinade to the pan and add the stock, hoisin sauce, brown sugar, and the remaining tamari sauce, lemon juice, and cornstarch. Mix well. Put the pan in the frying basket and Air Fry for 5-8 minutes or until bubbling and thick, stirring once. Remove and set aside. Put the chicken in the frying basket and Fry for 15-18 minutes, shaking the basket once. Remove the chicken to the sauce in the pan and return to the fryer to reheat for 2 minutes. Sprinkle with the sesame seeds and serve.

Maewoon Chicken Legs

Servings: 4
Cooking Time: 30 Minutes + Chilling Time
Ingredients:

- 4 scallions, sliced, whites and greens separated
- ¼ cup tamari
- 2 tbsp sesame oil
- 1 tsp sesame seeds
- ¼ cup honey
- 2 tbsp gochujang
- 2 tbsp ketchup
- 4 cloves garlic, minced
- ½ tsp ground ginger
- Salt and pepper to taste
- 1 tbsp parsley
- 1 ½ lb chicken legs

Directions:

1. Whisk all ingredients, except chicken and scallion greens, in a bowl. Reserve ¼ cup of marinade. Toss chicken legs in the remaining marinade and chill for 30 minutes.
2. Preheat air fryer at 400°F. Place chicken legs in the greased frying basket and Air Fry for 10 minutes. Turn chicken. Cook for 8 more minutes. Let sit in a serving dish for 5 minutes. Coat the cooked chicken with the reserved marinade and scatter with scallion greens, sesame seeds and parsley to serve.

Fish And Seafood Recipes

Five Spice Red Snapper With Green Onions And Orange Salsa

Servings: 2
Cooking Time: 8 Minutes
Ingredients:

- 2 oranges, peeled, segmented and chopped
- 1 tablespoon minced shallot
- 1 to 3 teaspoons minced red Jalapeño or Serrano pepper
- 1 tablespoon chopped fresh cilantro
- lime juice, to taste
- salt, to taste
- 2 (5- to 6-ounce) red snapper fillets
- ½ teaspoon Chinese five spice powder
- salt and freshly ground black pepper
- vegetable or olive oil, in a spray bottle
- 4 green onions, cut into 2-inch lengths

Directions:
1. Start by making the salsa. Cut the peel off the oranges, slicing around the oranges to expose the flesh. Segment the oranges by cutting in between the membranes of the orange. Chop the segments roughly and combine in a bowl with the shallot, Jalapeño or Serrano pepper, cilantro, lime juice and salt. Set the salsa aside.
2. Preheat the air fryer to 400°F.
3. Season the fish fillets with the five-spice powder, salt and freshly ground black pepper. Spray both sides of the fish fillets with oil. Toss the green onions with a little oil.
4. Transfer the fish to the air fryer basket and scatter the green onions around the fish. Air-fry at 400°F for 8 minutes.
5. Remove the fish from the air fryer, along with the fried green onions. Serve with white rice and a spoonful of the salsa on top.

Fish Goujons With Tartar Sauce

Servings: 4
Cooking Time: 20 Minutes
Ingredients:

- ¼ cup flour
- Salt and pepper to taste
- ¼ tsp smoked paprika
- ¼ tsp dried oregano
- 1 tsp dried thyme
- 1 egg
- 4 haddock fillets
- 1 lemon, thinly sliced
- ½ cup tartar sauce

Directions:
1. Preheat air fryer to 400°F. Combine flour, salt, pepper, paprika, thyme, and oregano in a wide bowl. Whisk egg and 1 teaspoon water in another wide bowl. Slice each fillet into 4 strips. Dip the strips in the egg mixture. Then roll them in the flour mixture and coat completely. Arrange the fish strips on the greased frying basket. Air Fry for 4 minutes. Flip the fish and Air Fry for another 4 to 5 minutes until crisp. Serve warm with lemon slices and tartar sauce on the side and enjoy.

Shrimp, Chorizo And Fingerling Potatoes

Servings: 4
Cooking Time: 16 Minutes
Ingredients:

- ½ red onion, chopped into 1-inch chunks
- 8 fingerling potatoes, sliced into 1-inch slices or halved lengthwise
- 1 teaspoon olive oil
- salt and freshly ground black pepper
- 8 ounces raw chorizo sausage, sliced into 1-inch chunks
- 16 raw large shrimp, peeled, deveined and tails removed
- 1 lime
- ¼ cup chopped fresh cilantro
- chopped orange zest (optional)

Directions:

1. Preheat the air fryer to 380°F.
2. Combine the red onion and potato chunks in a bowl and toss with the olive oil, salt and freshly ground black pepper.
3. Transfer the vegetables to the air fryer basket and air-fry for 6 minutes, shaking the basket a few times during the cooking process.
4. Add the chorizo chunks and continue to air-fry for another 5 minutes.
5. Add the shrimp, season with salt and continue to air-fry, shaking the basket every once in a while, for another 5 minutes.
6. Transfer the tossed shrimp, chorizo and potato to a bowl and squeeze some lime juice over the top to taste. Toss in the fresh cilantro, orange zest and a drizzle of olive oil, and season again to taste.
7. Serve with a fresh green salad.

Lemon & Herb Crusted Salmon

Servings: 4
Cooking Time: 20 Minutes
Ingredients:

- 1/3 cup crushed potato chips
- 4 skinless salmon fillets
- 3 tbsp honey mustard
- ½ tsp lemon zest
- ½ tsp dried thyme
- ½ tsp dried basil
- ¼ cup panko bread crumbs
- 2 tbsp olive oil

Directions:

1. Preheat air fryer to 320°F. Place the salmon on a work surface. Mix together mustard, lemon zest, thyme, and basil in a small bowl. Spread on top of the salmon evenly. In a separate small bowl, mix together bread crumbs and potato chips before drizzling with olive oil. Place the salmon in the frying basket. Bake until the salmon is cooked through and the topping is crispy and brown, about 10 minutes. Serve hot and enjoy!

Cheese & Crab Stuffed Mushrooms

Servings: 2
Cooking Time: 30 Minutes
Ingredients:

- 6 oz lump crabmeat, shells discarded
- 6 oz mascarpone cheese, softened
- 2 jalapeño peppers, minced
- ¼ cup diced red onions
- 2 tsp grated Parmesan cheese
- 2 portobello mushroom caps
- 2 tbsp butter, divided
- ½ tsp prepared horseradish
- ¼ tsp Worcestershire sauce
- ¼ tsp smoked paprika
- Salt and pepper to taste
- ¼ cup bread crumbs

Directions:

1. Melt 1 tbsp of butter in a skillet over heat for 30 seconds. Add in onion and cook for 3 minutes until tender. Stir in mascarpone cheese, Parmesan cheese, horseradish, jalapeño peppers, Worcestershire sauce, paprika, salt and pepper and cook for 2 minutes until smooth. Fold in crabmeat. Spoon mixture into mushroom caps. Set aside.
2. Preheat air fryer at 350ºF. Microwave the remaining butter until melted. Stir in breadcrumbs. Scatter over stuffed mushrooms. Place mushrooms in the greased frying basket and Bake for 8 minutes. Serve immediately.

Sardinas Fritas

Servings: 2
Cooking Time: 15 Minutes
Ingredients:

- 2 cans boneless, skinless sardines in mustard sauce
- Salt and pepper to taste
- ½ cup bread crumbs
- 2 lemon wedges
- 1 tsp chopped parsley

Directions:

1. Preheat air fryer at 350ºF. Add breadcrumbs, salt and black pepper to a bowl. Roll sardines in the breadcrumbs to coat. Place them in the greased frying basket and Air Fry for 6 minutes, flipping once. Transfer them to a serving dish. Serve topped with parsley and lemon wedges.

Korean-style Fried Calamari

Servings:4
Cooking Time: 25 Minutes
Ingredients:
- 2 tbsp tomato paste
- 1 tbsp gochujang
- 1 tbsp lime juice
- 1 tsp lime zest
- 1 tsp smoked paprika
- ½ tsp salt
- 1 cup bread crumbs
- 1/3 lb calamari rings

Directions:
1. Preheat air fryer to 400ºF. Whisk tomato paste, gochujang, lime juice and zest, paprika, and salt in a bowl. In another bowl, add in the bread crumbs. Dredge calamari rings in the tomato mixture, shake off excess, then roll through the crumbs. Place calamari rings in the greased frying basket and Air Fry for 4-5 minutes, flipping once. Serve.

Chili Blackened Shrimp

Servings: 4
Cooking Time: 15 Minutes
Ingredients:
- 1 lb peeled shrimp, deveined
- 1 tsp paprika
- ½ tsp dried dill
- ½ tsp red chili flakes
- ½ lemon, juiced
- Salt and pepper to taste

Directions:
1. Preheat air fryer to 400°F. In a resealable bag, add shrimp, paprika, dill, red chili flakes, lemon juice, salt and pepper. Seal and shake well. Place the shrimp in the greased frying basket and Air Fry for 7-8 minutes, shaking the basket once until blackened. Let cool slightly and serve.

Mexican-style Salmon Stir-fry

Servings: 4
Cooking Time: 30 Minutes
Ingredients:
- 12 oz salmon fillets, cubed
- 1 red bell pepper, chopped
- 1 red onion, chopped
- 1 jalapeño pepper, minced
- ¼ cup salsa
- 2 tbsp tomato juice
- 2 tsp peanut oil
- 1 tsp chili powder
- 2 tbsp cilantro, chopped

Directions:
1. Preheat air fryer to 360°F. Mix salmon, bell pepper, onion, jalapeño, salsa, tomato juice, peanut oil, and chili powder in a bowl and put it into the air fryer. Air Fry for 12-14 minutes until the salmon is firm and the veggies are crispy and soft, stirring once. Serve topped with cilantro.

Southeast Asian-style Tuna Steaks

Servings: 4
Cooking Time: 20 Minutes
Ingredients:
- 1 stalk lemongrass, bent in half
- 4 tuna steaks
- 2 tbsp soy sauce
- 2 tsp sesame oil
- 2 tsp rice wine vinegar
- 1 tsp grated fresh ginger
- ⅛ tsp pepper
- 3 tbsp lemon juice
- 2 tbsp chopped cilantro
- 1 sliced red chili

Directions:
1. Preheat air fryer to 390°F. Place the tuna steak on a shallow plate. Mix together soy sauce, sesame oil, rice wine vinegar, and ginger in a small bowl. Pour over the tuna, rubbing the marinade gently into both sides of the fish. Marinate for about 10 minutes. Then sprinkle with pepper. Place the lemongrass in the frying basket and top with tuna steaks. Add the remaining lemon juice and 1 tablespoon of water in the pan below the basket. Bake until the tuna is cooked through, 8-10 minutes. Discard the lemongrass before topping with cilantro and red chili. Serve and enjoy!

Sinaloa Fish Fajitas

Servings: 4
Cooking Time: 30 Minutes
Ingredients:

- 1 lemon, thinly sliced
- 16 oz red snapper filets
- 1 tbsp olive oil
- 1 tbsp cayenne pepper
- ½ tsp salt
- 2 cups shredded coleslaw

- 1 carrot, shredded
- 2 tbsp orange juice
- ½ cup salsa
- 4 flour tortillas
- ½ cup sour cream
- 2 avocados, sliced

Directions:

1. Preheat the air fryer to 350°F. Lay the lemon slices at the bottom of the basket. Drizzle the fillets with olive oil and sprinkle with cayenne pepper and salt. Lay the fillets on top of the lemons and Bake for 6-9 minutes or until the fish easily flakes. While the fish cooks, toss the coleslaw, carrot, orange juice, and salsa in a bowl. When the fish is done, remove it and cover. Toss the lemons. Air Fry the tortillas for 2-3 minutes to warm up. Add the fish to the tortillas and top with a cabbage mix, sour cream, and avocados. Serve and enjoy!

Sriracha Salmon Melt Sandwiches

Servings: 4
Cooking Time: 20 Minutes
Ingredients:

- 2 tbsp butter, softened
- 2 cans pink salmon
- 2 English muffins
- 1/3 cup mayonnaise
- 2 tbsp Dijon mustard

- 1 tbsp fresh lemon juice
- 1/3 cup chopped celery
- ½ tsp sriracha sauce
- 4 slices tomato
- 4 slices Swiss cheese

Directions:

1. Preheat the air fryer to 370°F. Split the English muffins with a fork and spread butter on the 4 halves. Put the halves in the basket and Bake for 3-5 minutes, or until toasted. Remove and set aside. Combine the salmon, mayonnaise, mustard, lemon juice, celery, and sriracha in a bowl. Divide among the English muffin halves. Top each sandwich with tomato and cheese and put in the frying basket. Bake for 4-6 minutes or until the cheese is melted and starts to brown. Serve hot.

Coconut Shrimp

Servings: 4
Cooking Time: 12 Minutes
Ingredients:

- 1 pound large shrimp (about 16 to 20), peeled and de-veined
- ½ cup flour
- salt and freshly ground black pepper
- 2 egg whites
- ½ cup fine breadcrumbs
- ½ cup shredded unsweetened coconut
- zest of one lime
- ½ teaspoon salt
- ⅛ to ¼ teaspoon ground cayenne pepper
- vegetable or canola oil
- sweet chili sauce or duck sauce (for serving)

Directions:
1. Set up a dredging station. Place the flour in a shallow dish and season well with salt and freshly ground black pepper. Whisk the egg whites in a second shallow dish. In a third shallow dish, combine the breadcrumbs, coconut, lime zest, salt and cayenne pepper.
2. Preheat the air fryer to 400°F.
3. Dredge each shrimp first in the flour, then dip it in the egg mixture, and finally press it into the breadcrumb-coconut mixture to coat all sides. Place the breaded shrimp on a plate or baking sheet and spray both sides with vegetable oil.
4. Air-fry the shrimp in two batches, being sure not to over-crowd the basket. Air-fry for 5 minutes, turning the shrimp over for the last minute or two. Repeat with the second batch of shrimp.
5. Lower the temperature of the air fryer to 340°F. Return the first batch of shrimp to the air fryer basket with the second batch and air-fry for an additional 2 minutes, just to re-heat everything.
6. Serve with sweet chili sauce, duck sauce or just eat them plain!

Almond Topped Trout

Servings: 4
Cooking Time: 20 Minutes
Ingredients:

- 4 trout fillets
- 2 tbsp olive oil
- Salt and pepper to taste
- 2 garlic cloves, sliced
- 1 lemon, sliced
- 1 tbsp flaked almonds

Directions:
1. Preheat air fryer to 380°F. Lightly brush each fillet with olive oil on both sides and season with salt and pepper. Put the fillets in a single layer in the frying basket. Put the sliced garlic over the tops of the trout fillets, then top with lemon slices and cook for 12-15 minutes. Serve topped with flaked almonds and enjoy!

Oyster Shrimp With Fried Rice

Servings: 4
Cooking Time: 40 Minutes
Ingredients:

- 1 lb peeled shrimp, deveined
- 1 shallot, chopped
- 2 garlic cloves, minced
- 1 tbsp olive oil
- 1 tbsp butter
- 2 eggs, beaten
- 2 cups cooked rice
- 1 cup baby peas
- 2 tbsp fish sauce
- 1 tbsp oyster sauce

Directions:

1. Preheat the air fryer to 370°F. Combine the shrimp, shallot, garlic, and olive oil in a cake pan. Put the cake pan in the air fryer and Bake the shrimp for 5-7 minutes, stirring once until shrimp are no pinker. Remove into a bowl, and set aside. Put the butter in the hot cake pan to melt. Add the eggs and return to the fryer. Bake for 4-6 minutes, stirring once until the eggs are set. Remove the eggs from the pan and set aside.
2. Add the rice, peas, oyster sauce, and fish sauce to the pan and return it to the fryer. Bake for 12-15 minutes, stirring once halfway through. Pour in the shrimp and eggs and stir. Cook for 2-3 more minutes until everything is hot.

Seared Scallops In Beurre Blanc

Servings: 4
Cooking Time: 15 Minutes
Ingredients:

- 1 lb sea scallops
- Salt and pepper to taste
- 2 tbsp butter, melted
- 1 lemon, zested and juiced
- 2 tbsp dry white wine

Directions:

1. Preheat the air fryer to 400°F. Sprinkle the scallops with salt and pepper, then set in a bowl. Combine the butter, lemon zest, lemon juice, and white wine in another bowl; mix well. Put the scallops in a baking pan and drizzle over them the mixture. Air Fry for 8-11 minutes, flipping over at about 5 minutes until opaque. Serve and enjoy!

Malaysian Shrimp With Sambal Mayo

Servings: 4
Cooking Time: 30 Minutes
Ingredients:

- 24 jumbo shrimp, peeled and deveined
- 2/3 cup panko bread crumbs
- 3 tbsp mayonnaise
- 1 tbsp sambal oelek paste
- 2/3 cup shredded coconut
- 1 lime, zested
- ½ tsp ground coriander
- Salt to taste
- 2 tbsp flour
- 2 eggs

Directions:

1. Mix together mayonnaise and sambal oelek in a bowl. Set aside. In another bowl, stir together coconut, lime, coriander, panko bread crumbs, and salt. In a shallow bowl, add flour. In another shallow bowl, whisk eggs until blended. Season shrimp with salt. First, dip the shrimp into the flour, shake, and dip into the egg mix. Dip again in the coconut mix. Gently press the coconut and panko to the shrimp. Preheat air fryer to 360°F. Put the shrimp in the greased frying basket and Air Fry for 8 minutes, flipping once until the crust is golden and the shrimp is cooked. Serve alongside the sweet chili mayo.

Fish Cakes

Servings: 4
Cooking Time: 10 Minutes
Ingredients:

- ¾ cup mashed potatoes (about 1 large russet potato)
- 12 ounces cod or other white fish
- salt and pepper
- oil for misting or cooking spray
- 1 large egg
- ¼ cup potato starch
- ½ cup panko breadcrumbs
- 1 tablespoon fresh chopped chives
- 2 tablespoons minced onion

Directions:

1. Peel potatoes, cut into cubes, and cook on stovetop till soft.
2. Salt and pepper raw fish to taste. Mist with oil or cooking spray, and cook in air fryer at 360°F for 6 to 8minutes, until fish flakes easily. If fish is crowded, rearrange halfway through cooking to ensure all pieces cook evenly.
3. Transfer fish to a plate and break apart to cool.
4. Beat egg in a shallow dish.
5. Place potato starch in another shallow dish, and panko crumbs in a third dish.
6. When potatoes are done, drain in colander and rinse with cold water.
7. In a large bowl, mash the potatoes and stir in the chives and onion. Add salt and pepper to taste, then stir in the fish.
8. If needed, stir in a tablespoon of the beaten egg to help bind the mixture.
9. Shape into 8 small, fat patties. Dust lightly with potato starch, dip in egg, and roll in panko crumbs. Spray both sides with oil or cooking spray.
10. Cook at 360°F for 10 minutes, until golden brown and crispy.

Tuna Patties With Dill Sauce

Servings: 6
Cooking Time: 10 Minutes
Ingredients:

- Two 5-ounce cans albacore tuna, drained
- ½ teaspoon garlic powder
- 2 teaspoons dried dill, divided
- ½ teaspoon black pepper
- ½ teaspoon salt, divided
- ¼ cup minced onion
- 1 large egg
- 7 tablespoons mayonnaise, divided
- ¼ cup panko breadcrumbs
- 1 teaspoon fresh lemon juice
- ¼ teaspoon fresh lemon zest
- 6 pieces butterleaf lettuce
- 1 cup diced tomatoes

Directions:

1. In a large bowl, mix the tuna with the garlic powder, 1 teaspoon of the dried dill, the black pepper, ¼ teaspoon of the salt, and the onion. Make sure to use the back of a fork to really break up the tuna so there are no large chunks.
2. Mix in the egg and 1 tablespoon of the mayonnaise; then fold in the breadcrumbs so the tuna begins to form a thick batter that holds together.
3. Portion the tuna mixture into 6 equal patties and place on a plate lined with parchment paper in the refrigerator for at least 30 minutes. This will help the patties hold together in the air fryer.
4. When ready to cook, preheat the air fryer to 350°F.
5. Liberally spray the metal trivet that sits inside the air fryer basket with olive oil mist and place the patties onto the trivet.
6. Cook for 5 minutes, flip, and cook another 5 minutes.
7. While the patties are cooking, make the dill sauce by combining the remaining 6 tablespoons of mayonnaise with the remaining 1 teaspoon of dill, the lemon juice, the lemon zest, and the remaining ¼ teaspoon of salt. Set aside.
8. Remove the patties from the air fryer.
9. Place 1 slice of lettuce on a plate and top with the tuna patty and a tomato slice. Repeat to form the remaining servings. Drizzle the dill dressing over the top. Serve immediately.

Perfect Soft-shelled Crabs

Servings:2
Cooking Time: 12 Minutes
Ingredients:

- ½ cup All-purpose flour
- 1 tablespoon Old Bay seasoning
- 1 Large egg(s), well beaten
- 1 cup (about 3 ounces) Ground oyster crackers
- 2 2½-ounce cleaned soft-shelled crab(s), about 4 inches across
- Vegetable oil spray

Directions:
1.   Preheat the air fryer to 375°F (or 380°F or 390°F, if one of these is the closest setting).
2.   Set up and fill three shallow soup plates or small pie plates on your counter: one for the flour, whisked with the Old Bay until well combined; one for the beaten egg(s); and one for the cracker crumbs.
3.   Set a soft-shelled crab in the flour mixture and turn to coat evenly and well on all sides, even inside the legs. Dip the crab into the egg(s) and coat well, turning at least once, again getting some of the egg between the legs. Let any excess egg slip back into the rest, then set the crab in the cracker crumbs. Turn several times, pressing very gently to get the crab evenly coated with crumbs, even between the legs. Generously coat the crab on all sides with vegetable oil spray. Set it aside if you're making more than one and coat these in the same way.
4.   Set the crab(s) in the basket with as much air space between them as possible. They may overlap slightly, particularly at the ends of their legs, depending on the basket's size. Air-fry undisturbed for 12 minutes, or until very crisp and golden brown. If the machine is at 390°F, the crabs may be done in only 10 minutes.
5.   Use kitchen tongs to gently transfer the crab(s) to a wire rack. Cool for a couple of minutes before serving.

Vegetable Side Dishes Recipes
Caraway Seed Pretzel Sticks

Servings: 4
Cooking Time: 30 Minutes
Ingredients:
- ½ pizza dough
- 1 tsp baking soda
- 2 tbsp caraway seeds

Directions:
1. Preheat air fryer to 400°F. Roll out the dough, on parchment paper, into a rectangle, then cut it into 8 strips.Whisk the baking soda and 1 cup of hot water until well dissolved in a bowl. Submerge each strip, shake off any excess, and stretch another 1 to 2 inches. Scatter with caraway seeds and let rise for 10 minutes in the frying basket. Grease with cooking spray and Air Fry for 8 minutes until golden brown, turning once. Serve.

Roast Sweet Potatoes With Parmesan

Servings: 4
Cooking Time: 30 Minutes
Ingredients:
- 2 peeled sweet potatoes, sliced
- ¼ cup grated Parmesan
- 1 tsp olive oil
- 1 tbsp balsamic vinegar
- 1 tsp dried rosemary

Directions:
1. Preheat air fryer to 400°F. Place the sweet potatoes and some olive oil in a bowl and shake to coat. Spritz with balsamic vinegar and rosemary, then shake again. Put the potatoes in the frying basket and Roast for 18-25 minutes, shaking at least once until the potatoes are soft. Sprinkle with Parmesan cheese and serve warm.

Roasted Brussels Sprouts With Bacon

Cooking Time: 20 Minutes
Servings: 4
Ingredients:
- 4 slices thick-cut bacon, chopped (about ¼ pound)
- 1 pound Brussels sprouts, halved (or quartered if large)
- freshly ground black pepper

Directions:
1. Preheat the air fryer to 380°F.
2. Air-fry the bacon for 5 minutes, shaking the basket once or twice during the cooking time.
3. Add the Brussels sprouts to the basket and drizzle a little bacon fat from the bottom of the air fryer drawer into the basket. Toss the sprouts to coat with the bacon fat. Air-fry for an additional 15 minutes, or until the Brussels sprouts are tender to a knifepoint.
4. Season with freshly ground black pepper.

Smooth & Silky Cauliflower Purée

Servings:4
Cooking Time: 25 Minutes
Ingredients:
- 1 head cauliflower, cut into florets
- 1 rutabaga, diced
- 4 tbsp butter, divided
- Salt and pepper to taste
- 3 cloves garlic, peeled
- 2 oz cream cheese, softened
- ½ cup milk
- 1 tsp dried thyme

Directions:
1. Preheat air fryer to 350ºF. Combine cauliflower, rutabaga, 2 tbsp of butter, and salt to taste in a bowl. Add veggie mixture to the frying basket and Air Fry for 10 minutes, tossing once. Put in garlic and Air Fry for 5 more minutes. Let them cool a bit, then transfer them to a blender. Blend them along with 2 tbsp of butter, salt, black pepper, cream cheese, thyme and milk until smooth. Serve immediately.

Honey-mustard Asparagus Puffs

Servings: 4
Cooking Time: 35 Minutes
Ingredients:

- 8 asparagus spears
- ½ sheet puff pastry
- 2 tbsp honey mustard
- 1 egg, lightly beaten

Directions:

1. Preheat the air fryer to 375°F. Spread the pastry with honey mustard and cut it into 8 strips. Wrap the pastry, honey mustard–side in, around the asparagus. Put a rack in the frying basket and lay the asparagus spears on the rack. Brush all over pastries with beaten egg and Air Fry for 12-17 minutes or until the pastry is golden. Serve.

Onions

Servings: 4
Cooking Time: 18 Minutes
Ingredients:

- 2 yellow onions (Vidalia or 1015 recommended)
- salt and pepper
- ¼ teaspoon ground thyme
- ¼ teaspoon smoked paprika
- 2 teaspoons olive oil
- 1 ounce Gruyère cheese, grated

Directions:

1. Peel onions and halve lengthwise (vertically).
2. Sprinkle cut sides of onions with salt, pepper, thyme, and paprika.
3. Place each onion half, cut-surface up, on a large square of aluminum foil. Pull sides of foil up to cup around onion. Drizzle cut surface of onions with oil.
4. Crimp foil at top to seal closed.
5. Place wrapped onions in air fryer basket and cook at 390°F for 18 minutes. When done, onions should be soft enough to pierce with fork but still slightly firm.
6. Open foil just enough to sprinkle each onion with grated cheese.
7. Cook for 30 seconds to 1 minute to melt cheese.

Layered Mixed Vegetables

Servings: 4
Cooking Time: 30 Minutes
Ingredients:

- 1 Yukon Gold potato, sliced
- 1 eggplant, sliced
- 1 carrot, thinly sliced
- ¼ cup minced onions
- 3 garlic cloves, minced
- ¾ cup milk
- 2 tbsp cornstarch
- ½ tsp dried thyme

Directions:

1. Preheat air fryer to 380°F. In layers, add the potato, eggplant, carrot, onion, and garlic to a baking pan. Combine the milk, cornstarch, and thyme in a bowl, then pour this mix over the veggies. Put the pan in the air fryer and Bake for 15 minutes. The casserole should be golden on top with softened veggies. Serve immediately.

Teriyaki Tofu With Spicy Mayo

Servings: 2
Cooking Time: 35 Minutes + 1 Hour To Marinate
Ingredients:

- 1 scallion, chopped
- 7 oz extra-firm tofu, sliced
- 2 tbsp soy sauce
- 1 tsp toasted sesame oil
- 1 red chili, thinly sliced
- 1 tsp mirin
- 1 tsp light brown sugar
- 1 garlic clove, grated
- ½ tsp grated ginger
- 1/3 cup sesame seeds
- 1 egg
- 4 tsp mayonnaise
- 1 tbsp lime juice
- 1 tsp hot chili powder

Directions:

1. Squeeze most of the water from the tofu by lightly pressing the slices between two towels. Place the tofu in a baking dish. Use a whisk to mix soy sauce, sesame oil, red chili, mirin, brown sugar, garlic and ginger. Pour half of the marinade over the tofu. Using a spatula, carefully flip the tofu down and pour the other half of the marinade over. Refrigerate for 1 hour.

2. Preheat air fryer to 400°F. In a shallow plate, add sesame seeds. In another shallow plate, beat the egg. Remove the tofu from the refrigerator. Let any excess marinade drip off. Dip each piece in the egg mixture and then in the sesame seeds. Transfer to greased frying basket. Air Fry for 10 minutes, flipping once until toasted and crispy. Meanwhile, mix mayonnaise, lime juice, and hot chili powder and in a small bowl. Top with a dollop of hot chili mayo and some scallions. Serve and enjoy!

Garlicky Bell Pepper Mix

Servings: 4
Cooking Time: 30 Minutes
Ingredients:

- 2 tbsp vegetable oil
- ½ tsp dried cilantro
- 1 red bell pepper
- 1 yellow bell pepper
- 1 orange bell pepper
- 1 green bell pepper
- Salt and pepper to taste
- 1 head garlic

Directions:

1.   Preheat air fryer to 330°F. Slice the peppers into 1-inch strips. Transfer them to a large bowl along with 1 tbsp of vegetable oil. Toss to coat. Season with cilantro, salt, and pepper. Cut the top of a garlic head and place it cut-side up on an oiled square of aluminium foil. Drizzle with vegetable oil and wrap completely in the foil.

2.   Roast the wrapped garlic in the air fryer for 15 minutes. Next, add the pepper strips and roast until the peppers are tender and the garlic is soft, 6-8 minutes. Transfer the peppers to a serving dish. Remove the garlic and unwrap the foil carefully. Once cooled, squeeze the cloves out of the garlic head and mix into the peppers' dish. Serve.

Sweet Roasted Pumpkin Rounds

Servings: 4
Cooking Time: 35 Minutes
Ingredients:

- 1 pumpkin
- 1 tbsp honey
- 1 tbsp melted butter
- ¼ tsp cardamom
- ¼ tsp sea salt

Directions:

1.   Preheat the air fryer to 370°F. Cut the pumpkin in half lengthwise and remove the seeds. Slice each half crosswise into 1-inch-wide half-circles, then cut each half-circle in half again to make quarter rounds. Combine the honey, butter, cardamom, and salt in a bowl and mix well. Toss the pumpkin in the mixture until coated, then put into the frying basket. Bake for 15-20 minutes, shaking once during cooking until the edges start to brown and the squash is tender.

Herby Roasted Cherry Tomatoes

Servings: 4
Cooking Time: 20 Minutes
Ingredients:

- 1 tbsp dried oregano
- 1 tbsp dried basil
- 2 tsp dried marjoram
- 1 tsp dried thyme
- 1 tsp salt
- 2 tbsp balsamic vinegar
- 20 cherry tomatoes
- 1 tbsp olive oil

Directions:
1. Preheat the air fryer to 400°F. Combine the oregano, basil, marjoram, thyme, and salt in a small bowl and mix well. Pout into a small glass jar. Poke each cherry tomato with a toothpick to prevent bursting. Put the tomatoes, balsamic vinegar and olive oil on a piece of aluminum foil and sprinkle with 1½ tsp of the herb mix; toss. Wrap the foil around the tomatoes, leaving air space in the packet, and seal loosely. Put the packet in the air fryer and Bake for 8-10 minutes or until the tomatoes are tender.

Latkes

Servings: 12
Cooking Time: 13 Minutes
Ingredients:

- 1 russet potato
- ¼ onion
- 2 eggs, lightly beaten
- ⅓ cup flour*
- ½ teaspoon baking powder
- 1 teaspoon salt
- freshly ground black pepper
- canola or vegetable oil, in a spray bottle
- chopped chives, for garnish
- apple sauce
- sour cream

Directions:
1. Shred the potato and onion with a coarse box grater or a food processor with the shredding blade. Place the shredded vegetables into a colander or mesh strainer and squeeze or press down firmly to remove the excess water.
2. Transfer the onion and potato to a large bowl and add the eggs, flour, baking powder, salt and black pepper. Mix to combine and then shape the mixture into patties, about ¼-cup of mixture each. Brush or spray both sides of the latkes with oil.
3. Preheat the air fryer to 400°F.
4. Air-fry the latkes in batches. Transfer one layer of the latkes to the air fryer basket and air-fry at 400°F for 12 to 13 minutes, flipping them over halfway through the cooking time. Transfer the finished latkes to a platter and cover with aluminum foil, or place them in a warm oven to keep warm.
5. Garnish the latkes with chopped chives and serve with sour cream and applesauce.

Sage Hasselback Potatoes

Servings: 4
Cooking Time: 45 Minutes
Ingredients:

- 1 lb fingerling potatoes
- 1 tbsp olive oil
- 1 tbsp butter
- 1tsp dried sage
- Salt and pepper to taste

Directions:

1. Preheat the air fryer to 400°F. Rinse the potatoes dry, then set them on a work surface and put two chopsticks lengthwise on either side of each so you won't cut all the way through. Make vertical, crosswise cuts in the potato, about ⅛ inch apart. Repeat with the remaining potatoes. Combine the olive oil and butter in a bowl and microwave for 30 seconds or until melted. Stir in the sage, salt, and pepper. Put the potatoes in a large bowl and drizzle with the olive oil mixture. Toss to coat, then put the potatoes in the fryer and Air Fry for 22-27 minutes, rearranging them after 10-12 minutes. Cook until the potatoes are tender. Serve hot and enjoy!

Stuffed Avocados

Servings: 4
Cooking Time: 8 Minutes
Ingredients:

- 1 cup frozen shoepeg corn, thawed
- 1 cup cooked black beans
- ¼ cup diced onion
- ½ teaspoon cumin
- 2 teaspoons lime juice, plus extra for serving
- salt and pepper
- 2 large avocados, split in half, pit removed

Directions:

1. Mix together the corn, beans, onion, cumin, and lime juice. Season to taste with salt and pepper.
2. Scoop out some of the flesh from center of each avocado and set aside. Divide corn mixture evenly between the cavities.
3. Set avocado halves in air fryer basket and cook at 360°F for 8 minutes, until corn mixture is hot.
4. Season the avocado flesh that you scooped out with a squirt of lime juice, salt, and pepper. Spoon it over the cooked halves.

Lemony Fried Fennel Slices

Servings:2
Cooking Time: 15 Minutes
Ingredients:
- 1 tbsp minced fennel fronds
- 1 fennel bulb
- 2 tsp olive oil
- ¼ tsp salt
- 2 lemon wedges
- 1 tsp fennel seeds

Directions:
1. Preheat air fryer to 350ºF. Remove the fronds from the fennel bulb and reserve them. Cut the fennel into thin slices. Rub fennel chips with olive oil on both sides and sprinkle with salt and fennel seeds. Place fennel slices in the frying basket and Bake for 8 minutes. Squeeze lemon on top and scatter with chopped fronds. Serve.

Simple Roasted Sweet Potatoes

Servings: 2
Cooking Time: 45 Minutes
Ingredients:
- 2 10- to 12-ounce sweet potato(es)

Directions:
1. Preheat the air fryer to 350°F .
2. Prick the sweet potato(es) in four or five different places with the tines of a flatware fork (not in a line but all around).
3. When the machine is at temperature, set the sweet potato(es) in the basket with as much air space between them as possible. Air-fry undisturbed for 45 minutes, or until soft when pricked with a fork.
4. Use kitchen tongs to transfer the sweet potato(es) to a wire rack. Cool for 5 minutes before serving.

Smoked Avocado Wedges

Servings:4
Cooking Time: 15 Minutes
Ingredients:
- ½ tsp smoked paprika
- 2 tsp olive oil
- ½ lime, juiced
- 8 peeled avocado wedges
- 1 tsp chipotle powder
- ¼ tsp salt

Directions:
1. Preheat air fryer to 400°F. Drizzle the avocado wedges with olive oil and lime juice. In a bowl, combine chipotle powder, smoked paprika, and salt. Sprinkle over the avocado wedges. Place them in the frying basket and Air Fry for 7 minutes. Serve immediately.

Roasted Thyme Asparagus

Servings: 4
Cooking Time: 20 Minutes
Ingredients:
- 1 lb asparagus, trimmed
- 2 tsp olive oil
- 3 garlic cloves, minced
- 2 tbsp balsamic vinegar
- ½ tsp dried thyme
- ½ red chili, finely sliced

Directions:
1. Preheat air fryer to 380°F. Put the asparagus and olive oil in a bowl and stir to coat, then put them in the frying basket. Toss some garlic over the asparagus and Roast for 4-8 minutes until crisp-tender. Spritz with balsamic vinegar and toss in some thyme leaves. Top with red chili slices and serve.

Simple Peppared Carrot Chips

Servings: 4
Cooking Time: 15 Minutes
Ingredients:
- 3 carrots, cut into coins
- 1 tbsp sesame oil
- Salt and pepper to taste

Directions:
1. Preheat air fryer at 375°F. Combine all ingredients in a bowl. Place carrots in the frying basket and Roast for 10 minutes, tossing once. Serve right away.

Roman Artichokes

Servings: 4
Cooking Time: 12 Minutes
Ingredients:
- 2 9-ounce box(es) frozen artichoke heart quarters, thawed
- 1½ tablespoons Olive oil
- 2 teaspoons Minced garlic
- 1 teaspoon Table salt
- Up to ½ teaspoon Red pepper flakes

Directions:
1. Preheat the air fryer to 400°F.
2. Gently toss the artichoke heart quarters, oil, garlic, salt, and red pepper flakes in a bowl until the quarters are well coated.
3. When the machine is at temperature, scrape the contents of the bowl into the basket. Spread the artichoke heart quarters out into as close to one layer as possible. Air-fry undisturbed for 8 minutes. Gently toss and rearrange the quarters so that any covered or touching parts are now exposed to the air currents, then air-fry undisturbed for 4 minutes more, until very crisp.
4. Gently pour the contents of the basket onto a wire rack. Cool for a few minutes before serving.

Vegetarians Recipes
Green Bean Sautée

Servings: 4
Cooking Time: 25 Minutes
Ingredients:

- 1 ½ lb green beans, trimmed
- 1 tbsp olive oil
- ½ tsp garlic powder
- Salt and pepper to taste
- 4 garlic cloves, thinly sliced
- 1 tbsp fresh basil, chopped

Directions:
1. Preheat the air fryer to 375°F. Toss the beans with the olive oil, garlic powder, salt, and pepper in a bowl, then add to the frying basket. Air Fry for 6 minutes, shaking the basket halfway through the cooking time. Add garlic to the air fryer and cook for 3-6 minutes or until the green beans are tender and the garlic slices start to brown. Sprinkle with basil and serve warm.

Pineapple & Veggie Souvlaki

Servings: 4
Cooking Time: 35 Minutes
Ingredients:

- 1 can pineapple rings in pineapple juice
- 1 red bell pepper, stemmed and seeded
- 1/3 cup butter
- 2 tbsp apple cider vinegar
- 2 tbsp hot sauce
- 1 tbsp allspice
- 1 tsp ground nutmeg
- 16 oz feta cheese
- 1 red onion, peeled
- 8 mushrooms, quartered

Directions:
1. Preheat air fryer to 400°F. Whisk the butter, pineapple juice, apple vinegar, hot sauce, allspice, and nutmeg until smooth. Set aside. Slice feta cheese into 16 cubes, then the bell pepper into 16 chunks, and finally red onion into 8 wedges, separating each wedge into 2 pieces.
2. Cut pineapple ring into quarters. Place veggie cubes and feta into the butter bowl and toss to coat. Thread the veggies, tofu, and pineapple onto 8 skewers, alternating 16 pieces on each skewer. Grill for 15 minutes until golden brown and cooked. Serve warm.

Spicy Vegetable And Tofu Shake Fry

Servings: 4
Cooking Time: 17 Minutes

Ingredients:

- 4 teaspoons canola oil, divided
- 2 tablespoons rice wine vinegar
- 1 tablespoon sriracha chili sauce
- ¼ cup soy sauce*
- ½ teaspoon toasted sesame oil
- 1 teaspoon minced garlic
- 1 tablespoon minced fresh ginger
- 8 ounces extra firm tofu
- ½ cup vegetable stock or water
- 1 tablespoon honey
- 1 tablespoon cornstarch
- ½ red onion, chopped
- 1 red or yellow bell pepper, chopped
- 1 cup green beans, cut into 2-inch lengths
- 4 ounces mushrooms, sliced
- 2 scallions, sliced
- 2 tablespoons fresh cilantro leaves
- 2 teaspoons toasted sesame seeds

Directions:

1.   Combine 1 tablespoon of the oil, vinegar, sriracha sauce, soy sauce, sesame oil, garlic and ginger in a small bowl. Cut the tofu into bite-sized cubes and toss the tofu in with the marinade while you prepare the other vegetables. When you are ready to start cooking, remove the tofu from the marinade and set it aside. Add the water, honey and cornstarch to the marinade and bring to a simmer on the stovetop, just until the sauce thickens. Set the sauce aside.

2.   Preheat the air fryer to 400°F.

3.   Toss the onion, pepper, green beans and mushrooms in a bowl with a little canola oil and season with salt. Air-fry at 400°F for 11 minutes, shaking the basket and tossing the vegetables every few minutes. When the vegetables are cooked to your preferred doneness, remove them from the air fryer and set aside.

4.   Add the tofu to the air fryer basket and air-fry at 400°F for 6 minutes, shaking the basket a few times during the cooking process. Add the vegetables back to the basket and air-fry for another minute. Transfer the vegetables and tofu to a large bowl, add the scallions and cilantro leaves and toss with the sauce. Serve over rice with sesame seeds sprinkled on top.

Rainbow Quinoa Patties

Servings: 4
Cooking Time: 20 Minutes
Ingredients:

- 1 cup canned tri-bean blend, drained and rinsed
- 2 tbsp olive oil
- ½ tsp ground cumin
- ½ tsp garlic salt
- 1 tbsp paprika
- 1/3 cup uncooked quinoa
- 2 tbsp chopped onion
- ¼ cup shredded carrot
- 2 tbsp chopped cilantro
- 1 tsp chili powder
- ½ tsp salt
- 2 tbsp mascarpone cheese

Directions:

1. Place 1/3 cup of water, 1 tbsp of olive oil, cumin, and salt in a saucepan over medium heat and bring it to a boil. Remove from the heat and stir in quinoa. Let rest covered for 5 minutes.
2. Preheat air fryer at 350ºF. Using the back of a fork, mash beans until smooth. Toss in cooked quinoa and the remaining ingredients. Form mixture into 4 patties. Place patties in the greased frying basket and Air Fry for 6 minutes, turning once, and brush with the remaining olive oil. Serve immediately.

Fried Rice With Curried Tofu

Servings:4
Cooking Time: 25 Minutes
Ingredients:

- 8 oz extra-firm tofu, cubed
- ½ cup canned coconut milk
- 2 tsp red curry paste
- 2 cloves garlic, minced
- 1 tbsp avocado oil
- 1 tbsp coconut oil
- 2 cups cooked rice
- 1 tbsp turmeric powder
- Salt and pepper to taste
- 4 lime wedges
- ¼ cup chopped cilantro

Directions:

1. Preheat air fryer to 350ºF. Combine tofu, coconut milk, curry paste, garlic, and avocado oil in a bowl. Pour the mixture into a baking pan. Place the pan in the frying basket and Air Fry for 10 minutes, stirring once.
2. Melt the coconut oil in a skillet over medium heat. Add in rice, turmeric powder, salt, and black pepper, and cook for 2 minutes or until heated through. Divide the cooked rice between 4 medium bowls and top with tofu mixture and sauce. Top with cilantro and lime wedges to serve.

Egg Rolls

Servings: 4
Cooking Time: 8 Minutes
Ingredients:

- 1 clove garlic, minced
- 1 teaspoon sesame oil
- 1 teaspoon olive oil
- ½ cup chopped celery
- ½ cup grated carrots
- 2 green onions, chopped
- 2 ounces mushrooms, chopped
- 2 cups shredded Napa cabbage
- 1 teaspoon low-sodium soy sauce
- 1 teaspoon cornstarch
- salt
- 1 egg
- 1 tablespoon water
- 4 egg roll wraps
- olive oil for misting or cooking spray

Directions:
1. In a large skillet, sauté garlic in sesame and olive oils over medium heat for 1 minute.
2. Add celery, carrots, onions, and mushrooms to skillet. Cook 1 minute, stirring.
3. Stir in cabbage, cover, and cook for 1 minute or just until cabbage slightly wilts.
4. In a small bowl, mix soy sauce and cornstarch. Stir into vegetables to thicken. Remove from heat. Salt to taste if needed.
5. Beat together egg and water in a small bowl.
6. Divide filling into 4 portions and roll up in egg roll wraps. Brush all over with egg wash to seal.
7. Mist egg rolls very lightly with olive oil or cooking spray and place in air fryer basket.
8. Cook at 390°F for 4minutes. Turn over and cook 4 more minutes, until golden brown and crispy.

Berbere Eggplant Dip

Servings:4
Cooking Time: 35 Minutes
Ingredients:

- 1 eggplant, halved lengthwise
- 3 tsp olive oil
- 2 tsp pine nuts
- ¼ cup tahini
- 1 tbsp lemon juice
- 2 cloves garlic, minced
- ¼ tsp berbere seasoning
- ⅛ tsp ground cumin
- Salt and pepper to taste
- 1 tbsp chopped parsley

Directions:
1. Preheat air fryer to 370°F. Brush the eggplant with some olive oil. With a fork, pierce the eggplant flesh a few times. Place them, flat sides-down, in the frying basket. Air Fry for 25 minutes. Transfer the eggplant to a cutting board and let cool for 3 minutes until easy to handle. Place pine nuts in the frying basket and Air Fry for 2 minutes, shaking every 30 seconds. Set aside in a bowl.
2. Scoop out the eggplant flesh and add to a food processor. Add in tahini, lemon juice, garlic, berbere seasoning, cumin, salt, and black pepper and pulse until smooth. Transfer to a serving bowl. Scatter with toasted pine nuts, parsley, and the remaining olive oil. Serve immediately.

Vegetable Hand Pies

Servings: 8
Cooking Time: 10 Minutes Per Batch
Ingredients:

- ¾ cup vegetable broth
- 8 ounces potatoes
- ¾ cup frozen chopped broccoli, thawed
- ¼ cup chopped mushrooms
- 1 tablespoon cornstarch
- 1 tablespoon milk
- 1 can organic flaky biscuits (8 large biscuits)
- oil for misting or cooking spray

Directions:

1. Place broth in medium saucepan over low heat.
2. While broth is heating, grate raw potato into a bowl of water to prevent browning. You will need ¾ cup grated potato.
3. Roughly chop the broccoli.
4. Drain potatoes and put them in the broth along with the broccoli and mushrooms. Cook on low for 5 minutes.
5. Dissolve cornstarch in milk, then stir the mixture into the broth. Cook about a minute, until mixture thickens a little. Remove from heat and cool slightly.
6. Separate each biscuit into 2 rounds. Divide vegetable mixture evenly over half the biscuit rounds, mounding filling in the center of each.
7. Top the four rounds with filling, then the other four rounds and crimp the edges together with a fork.
8. Spray both sides with oil or cooking spray and place 4 pies in a single layer in the air fryer basket.
9. Cook at 330°F for approximately 10 minutes.
10. Repeat with the remaining biscuits. The second batch may cook more quickly because the fryer will be hot.

Quinoa Burgers With Feta Cheese And Dill

Servings: 6
Cooking Time: 10 Minutes
Ingredients:

- 1 cup quinoa (red, white or multi-colored)
- 1½ cups water
- 1 teaspoon salt
- freshly ground black pepper
- 1½ cups rolled oats
- 3 eggs, lightly beaten
- ¼ cup minced white onion
- ½ cup crumbled feta cheese
- ¼ cup chopped fresh dill
- salt and freshly ground black pepper
- vegetable or canola oil, in a spray bottle
- whole-wheat hamburger buns (or gluten-free hamburger buns*)
- arugula
- tomato, sliced
- red onion, sliced
- mayonnaise

Directions:

1. Make the quinoa: Rinse the quinoa in cold water in a saucepan, swirling it with your hand until any dry husks rise to the surface. Drain the quinoa as well as you can and then put the saucepan on the stovetop to dry and toast the quinoa. Turn the heat to medium-high and shake the pan regularly until you see the quinoa moving easily and can hear the seeds moving in the pan, indicating that they are dry. Add the water, salt and pepper. Bring the liquid to a boil and then reduce the heat to low or medium-low. You should see just a few bubbles, not a boil. Cover with a lid, leaving it askew and simmer for 20 minutes. Turn the heat off and fluff the quinoa with a fork. If there's any liquid left in the bottom of the pot, place it back on the burner for another 3 minutes or so. Spread the cooked quinoa out on a sheet pan to cool.

2. Combine the room temperature quinoa in a large bowl with the oats, eggs, onion, cheese and dill. Season with salt and pepper and mix well (remember that feta cheese is salty). Shape the mixture into 6 patties with flat sides (so they fit more easily into the air fryer). Add a little water or a few more rolled oats if necessary to get the mixture to be the right consistency to make patties.

3. Preheat the air-fryer to 400°F.

4. Spray both sides of the patties generously with oil and transfer them to the air fryer basket in one layer (you will probably have to cook these burgers in batches, depending on the size of your air fryer). Air-fry each batch at 400°F for 10 minutes, flipping the burgers over halfway through the cooking time.

5. Build your burger on the whole-wheat hamburger buns with arugula, tomato, red onion and mayonnaise.

Quick-to-make Quesadillas

Servings: 4
Cooking Time: 30 Minutes
Ingredients:

- 12 oz goat cheese
- 2 tbsp vinegar
- 1 tbsp Taco seasoning
- 1 ripe avocado, pitted
- 4 scallions, finely sliced
- 2 tbsp lemon juice
- 4 flour tortillas
- ¼ cup hot sauce
- ½ cup Alfredo sauce
- 16 cherry tomatoes, halved

Directions:

1. Preheat air fryer to 400°F. Slice goat cheese into 4 pieces. Set aside. In a bowl, whisk vinegar and taco seasoning until combined. Submerge each slice into the vinegar and Air Fry for 12 minutes until crisp, turning once. Let cool slightly before cutting into 1/2-inch thick strips.
2. Using a fork, mash the avocado in a bowl. Stir in scallions and lemon juice and set aside. Lay one tortilla on a flat surface, cut from one edge to the center, then spread ¼ of the avocado mixture on one quadrant, 1 tbsp of hot sauce on the next quadrant, and finally 2 tbsp of Alfredo sauce on the other half. Top the non-sauce half with ¼ of cherry tomatoes and ¼ of goat cheese strips.
3. To fold, start with the avocado quadrant, folding each over the next one until you create a stacked triangle. Repeat the process with the remaining tortillas. Air Fry for 5 minutes until crispy, turning once. Serve warm.

Veggie-stuffed Bell Peppers

Servings:4
Cooking Time: 40 Minutes
Ingredients:

- ½ cup canned fire-roasted diced tomatoes, including juice
- 2 red bell peppers
- 4 tsp olive oil
- ½ yellow onion, diced
- 1 zucchini, diced
- ¾ cup chopped mushrooms
- ¼ cup tomato sauce
- 2 tsp Italian seasoning
- ¼ tsp smoked paprika
- Salt and pepper to taste

Directions:

1. Cut bell peppers in half from top to bottom and discard the seeds. Brush inside and tops of the bell peppers with some olive oil. Set aside. Warm the remaining olive oil in a skillet over medium heat. Stir-fry the onion, zucchini, and mushrooms for 5 minutes until the onions are tender. Combine tomatoes and their juice, tomato sauce, Italian seasoning, paprika, salt, and pepper in a bowl.
2. Preheat air fryer to 350ºF. Divide both mixtures between bell pepper halves. Place bell pepper halves in the frying basket and Air Fry for 8 minutes. Serve immediately.

Mushroom Lasagna

Servings: 4
Cooking Time: 40 Minutes
Ingredients:

- 2 tbsp olive oil
- 1 zucchini, diced
- ½ cup diced mushrooms
- ¼ cup diced onion
- 1 cup marinara sauce
- 1 cup ricotta cheese
- 1/3 cup grated Parmesan
- 1 egg
- 2 tsp Italian seasoning
- 2 tbsp fresh basil, chopped
- ½ tsp thyme
- 1 tbsp red pepper flakes
- ½ tsp salt
- 5 lasagna noodle sheets
- 1 cup grated mozzarella

Directions:

1. Heat the oil in a skillet over medium heat. Add zucchini, mushrooms, 1 tbsp of basil, thyme, red pepper flakes and onion and cook for 4 minutes until the veggies are tender. Toss in marinara sauce, and bring it to a bowl. Then, low the heat and simmer for 3 minutes.

2. Preheat air fryer at 375ºF. Combine ricotta cheese, Parmesan cheese, egg, Italian seasoning, and salt in a bowl. Spoon ¼ of the veggie mixture into a cake pan. Add a layer of lasagna noodles on top, breaking apart noodles first to fit pan. Then, top with 1/3 of ricotta mixture and ¼ of mozzarella cheese. Repeat the layer 2 more times, finishing with mozzarella cheese on top. Cover cake pan with aluminum foil.

3. Place cake pan in the frying basket and Bake for 12 minutes. Remove the foil and cook for 3 more minutes. Let rest for 10 minutes before slicing. Serve immediately sprinkled with the remaining fresh basil.

Crispy Apple Fries With Caramel Sauce

Servings: 4
Cooking Time: 15 Minutes
Ingredients:

- 4 medium apples, cored
- ¼ tsp cinnamon
- ¼ tsp nutmeg
- 1 cup caramel sauce

Directions:

1. Preheat air fryer to 350°F. Slice the apples to a 1/3-inch thickness for a crunchy chip. Place in a large bowl and sprinkle with cinnamon and nutmeg. Place the slices in the air fryer basket. Bake for 6 minutes. Shake the basket, then cook for another 4 minutes or until crunchy. Serve drizzled with caramel sauce and enjoy!

Tomato & Squash Stuffed Mushrooms

Servings:2
Cooking Time: 15 Minutes
Ingredients:

- 12 whole white button mushrooms
- 3 tsp olive oil
- 2 tbsp diced zucchini
- 1 tsp soy sauce
- ¼ tsp salt
- 2 tbsp tomato paste
- 1 tbsp chopped parsley

Directions:
1. Preheat air fryer to 350ºF. Remove the stems from the mushrooms. Chop the stems finely and set in a bowl. Brush 1 tsp of olive oil around the top ridge of mushroom caps. To the bowl of the stem, add all ingredients, except for parsley, and mix. Divide and press mixture into tops of mushroom caps. Place the mushrooms in the frying basket and Air Fry for 5 minutes. Top with parsley. Serve.

Spicy Sesame Tempeh Slaw With Peanut Dressing

Servings: 2
Cooking Time: 8 Minutes
Ingredients:

- 2 cups hot water
- 1 teaspoon salt
- 8 ounces tempeh, sliced into 1-inch-long pieces
- 2 tablespoons low-sodium soy sauce
- 2 tablespoons rice vinegar
- 1 tablespoon filtered water
- 2 teaspoons sesame oil
- ½ teaspoon fresh ginger
- 1 clove garlic, minced
- ¼ teaspoon black pepper
- ½ jalapeño, sliced
- 4 cups cabbage slaw
- 4 tablespoons Peanut Dressing (see the following recipe)
- 2 tablespoons fresh chopped cilantro
- 2 tablespoons chopped peanuts

Directions:
1. Mix the hot water with the salt and pour over the tempeh in a glass bowl. Stir and cover with a towel for 10 minutes.
2. Discard the water and leave the tempeh in the bowl.
3. In a medium bowl, mix the soy sauce, rice vinegar, filtered water, sesame oil, ginger, garlic, pepper, and jalapeño. Pour over the tempeh and cover with a towel. Place in the refrigerator to marinate for at least 2 hours.
4. Preheat the air fryer to 370°F. Remove the tempeh from the bowl and discard the remaining marinade.
5. Liberally spray the metal trivet that goes into the air fryer basket and place the tempeh on top of the trivet.
6. Cook for 4 minutes, flip, and cook another 4 minutes.
7. In a large bowl, mix the cabbage slaw with the Peanut Dressing and toss in the cilantro and chopped peanuts.
8. Portion onto 4 plates and place the cooked tempeh on top when cooking completes. Serve immediately.

Spaghetti Squash And Kale Fritters With Pomodoro Sauce

Servings: 3
Cooking Time: 45 Minutes

Ingredients:

- 1½-pound spaghetti squash (about half a large or a whole small squash)
- olive oil
- ½ onion, diced
- ½ red bell pepper, diced
- 2 cloves garlic, minced
- 4 cups coarsely chopped kale
- salt and freshly ground black pepper
- 1 egg
- ⅓ cup breadcrumbs, divided*
- ⅓ cup grated Parmesan cheese
- ½ teaspoon dried rubbed sage
- pinch nutmeg
- Pomodoro Sauce:
- 2 tablespoons olive oil
- ½ onion, chopped
- 1 to 2 cloves garlic, minced
- 1 (28-ounce) can peeled tomatoes
- ¼ cup red wine
- 1 teaspoon Italian seasoning
- 2 tablespoons chopped fresh basil, plus more for garnish
- salt and freshly ground black pepper
- ½ teaspoon sugar (optional)

Directions:

1. Preheat the air fryer to 370°F.
2. Cut the spaghetti squash in half lengthwise and remove the seeds. Rub the inside of the squash with olive oil and season with salt and pepper. Place the squash, cut side up, into the air fryer basket and air-fry for 30 minutes, flipping the squash over halfway through the cooking process.
3. While the squash is cooking, Preheat a large sauté pan over medium heat on the stovetop. Add a little olive oil and sauté the onions for 3 minutes, until they start to soften. Add the red pepper and garlic and continue to sauté for an additional 4 minutes. Add the kale and season with salt and pepper. Cook for 2 more minutes, or until the kale is soft. Transfer the mixture to a large bowl and let it cool.
4. While the squash continues to cook, make the Pomodoro sauce. Preheat the large sauté pan again over medium heat on the stovetop. Add the olive oil and sauté the onion and garlic for 2 to 3 minutes, until the onion begins to soften. Crush the canned tomatoes with your hands and add them to the pan along with the red wine and Italian seasoning and simmer for 20 minutes. Add the basil and season to taste with salt, pepper and sugar (if using).
5. When the spaghetti squash has finished cooking, use a fork to scrape the inside flesh of the squash onto a sheet pan. Spread the squash out and let it cool.
6. Once cool, add the spaghetti squash to the kale mixture, along with the egg, breadcrumbs, Parmesan cheese, sage, nutmeg, salt and freshly ground black pepper. Stir to combine well and then divide the mixture into 6 thick portions. You can shape the portions into patties, but I prefer to keep them a little random and unique in shape. Spray or brush the fritters with olive oil.
7. Preheat the air fryer to 370°F.
8. Brush the air fryer basket with a little olive oil and transfer the fritters to the basket. Air-fry the squash and kale fritters at 370°F for 15 minutes, flipping them over halfway through the cooking process.
9. Serve the fritters warm with the Pomodoro sauce spooned over the top or pooled on your plate. Garnish with the fresh basil leaves.

Cheesy Veggie Frittata

Servings: 2
Cooking Time: 65 Minutes
Ingredients:

- 4 oz Bella mushrooms, chopped
- ¼ cup halved grape tomatoes
- 1 cup baby spinach
- 1/3 cup chopped leeks
- 1 baby carrot, chopped
- 4 eggs
- ½ cup grated cheddar
- 1 tbsp milk
- ¼ tsp garlic powder
- ¼ tsp dried oregano
- Salt and pepper to taste

Directions:

1. Preheat air fryer to 300°F. Crack the eggs into a bowl and beat them with a fork or whisk. Mix in the remaining ingredients until well combined. Pour into a greased cake pan. Put the pan into the frying basket and Bake for 20-23 minutes or until eggs are set in the center. Remove from the fryer. Cut into halves and serve.

Roasted Vegetable Thai Green Curry

Servings: 4
Cooking Time: 16 Minutes
Ingredients:

- 1 (13-ounce) can coconut milk
- 3 tablespoons green curry paste
- 1 tablespoon soy sauce*
- 1 tablespoon rice wine vinegar
- 1 teaspoon sugar
- 1 teaspoon minced fresh ginger
- ½ onion, chopped
- 3 carrots, sliced
- 1 red bell pepper, chopped
- olive oil
- 10 stalks of asparagus, cut into 2-inch pieces
- 3 cups broccoli florets
- basmati rice for serving
- fresh cilantro
- crushed red pepper flakes (optional)

Directions:

1. Combine the coconut milk, green curry paste, soy sauce, rice wine vinegar, sugar and ginger in a medium saucepan and bring to a boil on the stovetop. Reduce the heat and simmer for 20 minutes while you cook the vegetables. Set aside.
2. Preheat the air fryer to 400°F.
3. Toss the onion, carrots, and red pepper together with a little olive oil and transfer the vegetables to the air fryer basket. Air-fry at 400°F for 10 minutes, shaking the basket a few times during the cooking process. Add the asparagus and broccoli florets and air-fry for an additional 6 minutes, again shaking the basket for even cooking.
4. When the vegetables are cooked to your liking, toss them with the green curry sauce and serve in bowls over basmati rice. Garnish with fresh chopped cilantro and crushed red pepper flakes.

Mushroom, Zucchini And Black Bean Burgers

Servings: 4
Cooking Time: 18 Minutes
Ingredients:

- 1 cup diced zucchini, (about ½ medium zucchini)
- 1 tablespoon olive oil
- salt and freshly ground black pepper
- 1 cup chopped brown mushrooms (about 3 ounces)
- 1 small clove garlic
- 1 (15-ounce) can black beans, drained and rinsed
- 1 teaspoon lemon zest
- 1 tablespoon chopped fresh cilantro
- ½ cup plain breadcrumbs
- 1 egg, beaten
- ½ teaspoon salt
- freshly ground black pepper
- whole-wheat pita bread, burger buns or brioche buns
- mayonnaise, tomato, avocado and lettuce, for serving

Directions:

1. Preheat the air fryer to 400°F.
2. Toss the zucchini with the olive oil, season with salt and freshly ground black pepper and air-fry for 6 minutes, shaking the basket once or twice while it cooks.
3. Transfer the zucchini to a food processor with the mushrooms, garlic and black beans and process until still a little chunky but broken down and pasty. Transfer the mixture to a bowl. Add the lemon zest, cilantro, breadcrumbs and egg and mix well. Season again with salt and freshly ground black pepper. Shape the mixture into four burger patties and refrigerate for at least 15 minutes.
4. Preheat the air fryer to 370°F. Transfer two of the veggie burgers to the air fryer basket and air-fry for 12 minutes, flipping the burgers gently halfway through the cooking time. Keep the burgers warm by loosely tenting them with foil while you cook the remaining two burgers. Return the first batch of burgers back into the air fryer with the second batch for the last two minutes of cooking to re-heat.
5. Serve on toasted whole-wheat pita bread, burger buns or brioche buns with some mayonnaise, tomato, avocado and lettuce.

84

Vegan Buddha Bowls(1)

Servings: 2
Cooking Time: 45 Minutes
Ingredients:

- ½ cup quinoa
- 1 cup sweet potato cubes
- 12 oz broccoli florets
- ¾ cup bread crumbs
- ¼ cup chickpea flour
- ¼ cup hot sauce
- 16 oz super-firm tofu, cubed
- 1 tsp lemon juice
- 2 tsp olive oil
- Salt to taste
- 2 scallions, thinly sliced
- 1 tbsp sesame seeds

Directions:

1. Preheat air fryer to 400°F. Add quinoa and 1 cup of boiling water in a baking pan, cover it with aluminum foil, and Air Fry for 10 minutes. Set aside covered. Put the sweet potatoes in the basket and Air Fry for 2 minutes. Add in broccoli and Air Fry for 5 more minutes. Shake up and cook for another 3 minutes. Set the veggies aside.

2. On a plate, put the breadcrumbs. In a bowl, whisk chickpea flour and hot sauce. Toss in tofu cubes until coated and dip them in the breadcrumbs. Air Fry for 10 minutes until crispy. Share quinoa and fried veggies into 2 bowls. Top with crispy tofu and drizzle with lemon juice, olive oil and salt to taste. Scatter with scallions and sesame seeds before serving.

Sandwiches And Burgers Recipes
White Bean Veggie Burgers

Servings: 3
Cooking Time: 13 Minutes
Ingredients:

- 1⅓ cups Drained and rinsed canned white beans
- 3 tablespoons Rolled oats (not quick-cooking or steel-cut; gluten-free, if a concern)
- 3 tablespoons Chopped walnuts
- 2 teaspoons Olive oil
- 2 teaspoons Lemon juice
- 1½ teaspoons Dijon mustard (gluten-free, if a concern)
- ¾ teaspoon Dried sage leaves
- ¼ teaspoon Table salt
- Olive oil spray
- 3 Whole-wheat buns or gluten-free whole-grain buns (if a concern), split open

Directions:
1. Preheat the air fryer to 400°F.
2. Place the beans, oats, walnuts, oil, lemon juice, mustard, sage, and salt in a food processor. Cover and process to make a coarse paste that will hold its shape, about like wet sugar-cookie dough, stopping the machine to scrape down the inside of the canister at least once.
3. Scrape down and remove the blade. With clean and wet hands, form the bean paste into two 4-inch patties for the small batch, three 4-inch patties for the medium, or four 4-inch patties for the large batch. Generously coat the patties on both sides with olive oil spray.
4. Set them in the basket with some space between them and air-fry undisturbed for 12 minutes, or until lightly brown and crisp at the edges. The tops of the burgers will feel firm to the touch.
5. Use a nonstick-safe spatula, and perhaps a flatware fork for balance, to transfer the burgers to a cutting board. Set the buns cut side down in the basket in one layer (working in batches as necessary) and air-fry undisturbed for 1 minute, to toast a bit and warm up. Serve the burgers warm in the buns.

Chili Cheese Dogs

Servings: 3
Cooking Time: 12 Minutes
Ingredients:

- ¾ pound Lean ground beef
- 1½ tablespoons Chile powder
- 1 cup plus 2 tablespoons Jarred sofrito
- 3 Hot dogs (gluten-free, if a concern)
- 3 Hot dog buns (gluten-free, if a concern), split open lengthwise
- 3 tablespoons Finely chopped scallion
- 9 tablespoons (a little more than 2 ounces) Shredded Cheddar cheese

Directions:

1. Crumble the ground beef into a medium or large saucepan set over medium heat. Brown well, stirring often to break up the clumps. Add the chile powder and cook for 30 seconds, stirring the whole time. Stir in the sofrito and bring to a simmer. Reduce the heat to low and simmer, stirring occasionally, for 5 minutes. Keep warm.
2. Preheat the air fryer to 400°F.
3. When the machine is at temperature, put the hot dogs in the basket and air-fry undisturbed for 10 minutes, or until the hot dogs are bubbling and blistered, even a little crisp.
4. Use kitchen tongs to put the hot dogs in the buns. Top each with a ½ cup of the ground beef mixture, 1 tablespoon of the minced scallion, and 3 tablespoons of the cheese. (The scallion should go under the cheese so it superheats and wilts a bit.) Set the filled hot dog buns in the basket and air-fry undisturbed for 2 minutes, or until the cheese has melted.
5. Remove the basket from the machine. Cool the chili cheese dogs in the basket for 5 minutes before serving.

Crunchy Falafel Balls

Servings: 8
Cooking Time: 16 Minutes
Ingredients:

- 2½ cups Drained and rinsed canned chickpeas
- ¼ cup Olive oil
- 3 tablespoons All-purpose flour
- 1½ teaspoons Dried oregano
- 1½ teaspoons Dried sage leaves
- 1½ teaspoons Dried thyme
- ¾ teaspoon Table salt
- Olive oil spray

Directions:

1. Preheat the air fryer to 400°F.
2. Place the chickpeas, olive oil, flour, oregano, sage, thyme, and salt in a food processor. Cover and process into a paste, stopping the machine at least once to scrape down the inside of the canister.
3. Scrape down and remove the blade. Using clean, wet hands, form 2 tablespoons of the paste into a ball, then continue making 9 more balls for a small batch, 15 more for a medium one, and 19 more for a large batch. Generously coat the balls in olive oil spray.
4. Set the balls in the basket in one layer with a little space between them and air-fry undisturbed for 16 minutes, or until well browned and crisp.
5. Dump the contents of the basket onto a wire rack. Cool for 5 minutes before serving.

Provolone Stuffed Meatballs

Servings: 4
Cooking Time: 12 Minutes
Ingredients:
- 1 tablespoon olive oil
- 1 small onion, very finely chopped
- 1 to 2 cloves garlic, minced
- ¾ pound ground beef
- ¾ pound ground pork
- ¾ cup breadcrumbs
- ¼ cup grated Parmesan cheese
- ¼ cup finely chopped fresh parsley (or 1 tablespoon dried parsley)
- ½ teaspoon dried oregano
- 1½ teaspoons salt
- freshly ground black pepper
- 2 eggs, lightly beaten
- 5 ounces sharp or aged provolone cheese, cut into 1-inch cubes

Directions:
1. Preheat a skillet over medium-high heat. Add the oil and cook the onion and garlic until tender, but not browned.
2. Transfer the onion and garlic to a large bowl and add the beef, pork, breadcrumbs, Parmesan cheese, parsley, oregano, salt, pepper and eggs. Mix well until all the ingredients are combined. Divide the mixture into 12 evenly sized balls. Make one meatball at a time, by pressing a hole in the meatball mixture with your finger and pushing a piece of provolone cheese into the hole. Mold the meat back into a ball, enclosing the cheese.
3. Preheat the air fryer to 380°F.
4. Working in two batches, transfer six of the meatballs to the air fryer basket and air-fry for 12 minutes, shaking the basket and turning the meatballs a couple of times during the cooking process. Repeat with the remaining six meatballs. You can pop the first batch of meatballs into the air fryer for the last two minutes of cooking to re-heat them. Serve warm.

Inside-out Cheeseburgers

Servings: 3

Cooking Time: 9-11 Minutes

Ingredients:

- 1 pound 2 ounces 90% lean ground beef
- ¾ teaspoon Dried oregano
- ¾ teaspoon Table salt
- ¾ teaspoon Ground black pepper
- ¼ teaspoon Garlic powder
- 6 tablespoons (about 1½ ounces) Shredded Cheddar, Swiss, or other semi-firm cheese, or a purchased blend of shredded cheeses
- 3 Hamburger buns (gluten-free, if a concern), split open

Directions:

1. Preheat the air fryer to 375°F .

2. Gently mix the ground beef, oregano, salt, pepper, and garlic powder in a bowl until well combined without turning the mixture to mush. Form it into two 6-inch patties for the small batch, three for the medium, or four for the large.

3. Place 2 tablespoons of the shredded cheese in the center of each patty. With clean hands, fold the sides of the patty up to cover the cheese, then pick it up and roll it gently into a ball to seal the cheese inside. Gently press it back into a 5-inch burger without letting any cheese squish out. Continue filling and preparing more burgers, as needed.

4. Place the burgers in the basket in one layer and air-fry undisturbed for 8 minutes for medium or 10 minutes for well-done. (An instant-read meat thermometer won't work for these burgers because it will hit the mostly melted cheese inside and offer a hotter temperature than the surrounding meat.)

5. Use a nonstick-safe spatula, and perhaps a flatware fork for balance, to transfer the burgers to a cutting board. Set the buns cut side down in the basket in one layer (working in batches as necessary) and air-fry undisturbed for 1 minute, to toast a bit and warm up. Cool the burgers a few minutes more, then serve them warm in the buns.

Perfect Burgers

Servings: 3
Cooking Time: 13 Minutes
Ingredients:
- 1 pound 2 ounces 90% lean ground beef
- 1½ tablespoons Worcestershire sauce (gluten-free, if a concern)
- ½ teaspoon Ground black pepper
- 3 Hamburger buns (gluten-free if a concern), split open

Directions:
1. Preheat the air fryer to 375°F .
2. Gently mix the ground beef, Worcestershire sauce, and pepper in a bowl until well combined but preserving as much of the meat's fibers as possible. Divide this mixture into two 5-inch patties for the small batch, three 5-inch patties for the medium, or four 5-inch patties for the large. Make a thumbprint indentation in the center of each patty, about halfway through the meat.
3. Set the patties in the basket in one layer with some space between them. Air-fry undisturbed for 10 minutes, or until an instant-read meat thermometer inserted into the center of a burger registers 160°F (a medium-well burger). You may need to add 2 minutes cooking time if the air fryer is at 360°F.
4. Use a nonstick-safe spatula, and perhaps a flatware fork for balance, to transfer the burgers to a cutting board. Set the buns cut side down in the basket in one layer (working in batches as necessary) and air-fry undisturbed for 1 minute, to toast a bit and warm up. Serve the burgers in the warm buns.

Philly Cheesesteak Sandwiches

Servings: 3
Cooking Time: 9 Minutes
Ingredients:
- ¾ pound Shaved beef
- 1 tablespoon Worcestershire sauce (gluten-free, if a concern)
- ¼ teaspoon Garlic powder
- ¼ teaspoon Mild paprika
- 6 tablespoons (1½ ounces) Frozen bell pepper strips (do not thaw)
- 2 slices, broken into rings Very thin yellow or white medium onion slice(s)
- 6 ounces (6 to 8 slices) Provolone cheese slices
- 3 Long soft rolls such as hero, hoagie, or Italian sub rolls, or hot dog buns (gluten-free, if a concern), split open lengthwise

Directions:
1. Preheat the air fryer to 400°F.
2. When the machine is at temperature, spread the shaved beef in the basket, leaving a ½-inch perimeter around the meat for good air flow. Sprinkle the meat with the Worcestershire sauce, paprika, and garlic powder. Spread the peppers and onions on top of the meat.
3. Air-fry undisturbed for 6 minutes, or until cooked through. Set the cheese on top of the meat. Continue air-frying undisturbed for 3 minutes, or until the cheese has melted.
4. Use kitchen tongs to divide the meat and cheese layers in the basket between the rolls or buns. Serve hot.

Black Bean Veggie Burgers

Servings: 3
Cooking Time: 10 Minutes

Ingredients:

- 1 cup Drained and rinsed canned black beans
- ⅓ cup Pecan pieces
- ⅓ cup Rolled oats (not quick-cooking or steel-cut; gluten-free, if a concern)
- 2 tablespoons (or 1 small egg) Pasteurized egg substitute, such as Egg Beaters (gluten-free, if a concern)
- 2 teaspoons Red ketchup-like chili sauce, such as Heinz
- ¼ teaspoon Ground cumin
- ¼ teaspoon Dried oregano
- ¼ teaspoon Table salt
- ¼ teaspoon Ground black pepper
- Olive oil
- Olive oil spray

Directions:

1. Preheat the air fryer to 400°F.
2. Put the beans, pecans, oats, egg substitute or egg, chili sauce, cumin, oregano, salt, and pepper in a food processor. Cover and process to a coarse paste that will hold its shape like sugar-cookie dough, adding olive oil in 1-teaspoon increments to get the mixture to blend smoothly. The amount of olive oil is actually dependent on the internal moisture content of the beans and the oats. Figure on about 1 tablespoon (three 1-teaspoon additions) for the smaller batch, with proportional increases for the other batches. A little too much olive oil can't hurt, but a dry paste will fall apart as it cooks and a far-too-wet paste will stick to the basket.
3. Scrape down and remove the blade. Using clean, wet hands, form the paste into two 4-inch patties for the small batch, three 4-inch patties for the medium, or four 4-inch patties for the large batch, setting them one by one on a cutting board. Generously coat both sides of the patties with olive oil spray.
4. Set them in the basket in one layer. Air-fry undisturbed for 10 minutes, or until lightly browned and crisp at the edges.
5. Use a nonstick-safe spatula, and perhaps a flatware fork for balance, to transfer the burgers to a wire rack. Cool for 5 minutes before serving.

Chicken Club Sandwiches

Servings: 3

Cooking Time: 15 Minutes

Ingredients:

- 3 5- to 6-ounce boneless skinless chicken breasts
- 6 Thick-cut bacon strips (gluten-free, if a concern)
- 3 Long soft rolls, such as hero, hoagie, or Italian sub rolls (gluten-free, if a concern)
- 3 tablespoons Regular, low-fat, or fat-free mayonnaise (gluten-free, if a concern)
- 3 Lettuce leaves, preferably romaine or iceberg
- 6 ¼-inch-thick tomato slices

Directions:

1. Preheat the air fryer to 375°F .
2. Wrap each chicken breast with 2 strips of bacon, spiraling the bacon around the meat, slightly overlapping the strips on each revolution. Start the second strip of bacon farther down the breast but on a line with the start of the first strip so they both end at a lined-up point on the chicken breast.
3. When the machine is at temperature, set the wrapped breasts bacon-seam side down in the basket with space between them. Air-fry undisturbed for 12 minutes, until the bacon is browned, crisp, and cooked through and an instant-read meat thermometer inserted into the center of a breast registers 165°F. You may need to add 2 minutes in the air fryer if the temperature is at 360°F.
4. Use kitchen tongs to transfer the breasts to a wire rack. Split the rolls open lengthwise and set them cut side down in the basket. Air-fry for 1 minute, or until warmed through.
5. Use kitchen tongs to transfer the rolls to a cutting board. Spread 1 tablespoon mayonnaise on the cut side of one half of each roll. Top with a chicken breast, lettuce leaf, and tomato slice. Serve warm.

Best-ever Roast Beef Sandwiches

Servings: 6
Cooking Time: 30-50 Minutes
Ingredients:

- 2½ teaspoons Olive oil
- 1½ teaspoons Dried oregano
- 1½ teaspoons Dried thyme
- 1½ teaspoons Onion powder
- 1½ teaspoons Table salt
- 1½ teaspoons Ground black pepper
- 3 pounds Beef eye of round
- 6 Round soft rolls, such as Kaiser rolls or hamburger buns (gluten-free, if a concern), split open lengthwise
- ¾ cup Regular, low-fat, or fat-free mayonnaise (gluten-free, if a concern)
- 6 Romaine lettuce leaves, rinsed
- 6 Round tomato slices (¼ inch thick)

Directions:

1. Preheat the air fryer to 350°F .
2. Mix the oil, oregano, thyme, onion powder, salt, and pepper in a small bowl. Spread this mixture all over the eye of round.
3. When the machine is at temperature, set the beef in the basket and air-fry for 30 to 50 minutes (the range depends on the size of the cut), turning the meat twice, until an instant-read meat thermometer inserted into the thickest piece of the meat registers 130°F for rare, 140°F for medium, or 150°F for well-done.
4. Use kitchen tongs to transfer the beef to a cutting board. Cool for 10 minutes. If serving now, carve into ⅛-inch-thick slices. Spread each roll with 2 tablespoons mayonnaise and divide the beef slices between the rolls. Top with a lettuce leaf and a tomato slice and serve. Or set the beef in a container, cover, and refrigerate for up to 3 days to make cold roast beef sandwiches anytime.

Chicken Saltimbocca Sandwiches

Servings: 3
Cooking Time: 11 Minutes
Ingredients:

- 3 5- to 6-ounce boneless skinless chicken breasts
- 6 Thin prosciutto slices
- 6 Provolone cheese slices
- 3 Long soft rolls, such as hero, hoagie, or Italian sub rolls (gluten-free, if a concern), split open lengthwise
- 3 tablespoons Pesto, purchased or homemade (see the headnote)

Directions:
1. Preheat the air fryer to 400°F.
2. Wrap each chicken breast with 2 prosciutto slices, spiraling the prosciutto around the breast and overlapping the slices a bit to cover the breast. The prosciutto will stick to the chicken more readily than bacon does.
3. When the machine is at temperature, set the wrapped chicken breasts in the basket and air-fry undisturbed for 10 minutes, or until the prosciutto is frizzled and the chicken is cooked through.
4. Overlap 2 cheese slices on each breast. Air-fry undisturbed for 1 minute, or until melted. Take the basket out of the machine.
5. Smear the insides of the rolls with the pesto, then use kitchen tongs to put a wrapped and cheesy chicken breast in each roll.

Eggplant Parmesan Subs

Servings: 2
Cooking Time: 13 Minutes
Ingredients:

- 4 Peeled eggplant slices (about ½ inch thick and 3 inches in diameter)
- Olive oil spray
- 2 tablespoons plus 2 teaspoons Jarred pizza sauce, any variety except creamy
- ¼ cup (about ⅔ ounce) Finely grated Parmesan cheese
- 2 Small, long soft rolls, such as hero, hoagie, or Italian sub rolls (gluten-free, if a concern), split open lengthwise

Directions:
1. Preheat the air fryer to 350°F .
2. When the machine is at temperature, coat both sides of the eggplant slices with olive oil spray. Set them in the basket in one layer and air-fry undisturbed for 10 minutes, until lightly browned and softened.
3. Increase the machine's temperature to 375°F (or 370°F, if that's the closest setting—unless the machine is already at 360°F, in which case leave it alone). Top each eggplant slice with 2 teaspoons pizza sauce, then 1 tablespoon cheese. Air-fry undisturbed for 2 minutes, or until the cheese has melted.
4. Use a nonstick-safe spatula, and perhaps a flatware fork for balance, to transfer the eggplant slices cheese side up to a cutting board. Set the roll(s) cut side down in the basket in one layer (working in batches as necessary) and air-fry undisturbed for 1 minute, to toast the rolls a bit and warm them up. Set 2 eggplant slices in each warm roll.

Dijon Thyme Burgers

Servings: 3
Cooking Time: 18 Minutes
Ingredients:

- 1 pound lean ground beef
- ⅓ cup panko breadcrumbs
- ¼ cup finely chopped onion
- 3 tablespoons Dijon mustard
- 1 tablespoon chopped fresh thyme
- 4 teaspoons Worcestershire sauce
- 1 teaspoon salt
- freshly ground black pepper
- Topping (optional):
- 2 tablespoons Dijon mustard
- 1 tablespoon dark brown sugar
- 1 teaspoon Worcestershire sauce
- 4 ounces sliced Swiss cheese, optional

Directions:
1. Combine all the burger ingredients together in a large bowl and mix well. Divide the meat into 4 equal portions and then form the burgers, being careful not to over-handle the meat. One good way to do this is to throw the meat back and forth from one hand to another, packing the meat each time you catch it. Flatten the balls into patties, making an indentation in the center of each patty with your thumb (this will help it stay flat as it cooks) and flattening the sides of the burgers so that they will fit nicely into the air fryer basket.
2. Preheat the air fryer to 370°F.
3. If you don't have room for all four burgers, air-fry two or three burgers at a time for 8 minutes. Flip the burgers over and air-fry for another 6 minutes.
4. While the burgers are cooking combine the Dijon mustard, dark brown sugar, and Worcestershire sauce in a small bowl and mix well. This optional topping to the burgers really adds a boost of flavor at the end. Spread the Dijon topping evenly on each burger. If you cooked the burgers in batches, return the first batch to the cooker at this time – it's ok to place the fourth burger on top of the others in the center of the basket. Air-fry the burgers for another 3 minutes.
5. Finally, if desired, top each burger with a slice of Swiss cheese. Lower the air fryer temperature to 330°F and air-fry for another minute to melt the cheese. Serve the burgers on toasted brioche buns, dressed the way you like them.

Asian Glazed Meatballs

Servings: 4

Cooking Time: 10 Minutes

Ingredients:

- 1 large shallot, finely chopped
- 2 cloves garlic, minced
- 1 tablespoon grated fresh ginger
- 2 teaspoons fresh thyme, finely chopped
- 1½ cups brown mushrooms, very finely chopped (a food processor works well here)
- 2 tablespoons soy sauce
- freshly ground black pepper
- 1 pound ground beef
- ½ pound ground pork
- 3 egg yolks
- 1 cup Thai sweet chili sauce (spring roll sauce)
- ¼ cup toasted sesame seeds
- 2 scallions, sliced

Directions:

1. Combine the shallot, garlic, ginger, thyme, mushrooms, soy sauce, freshly ground black pepper, ground beef and pork, and egg yolks in a bowl and mix the ingredients together. Gently shape the mixture into 24 balls, about the size of a golf ball.

2. Preheat the air fryer to 380°F.

3. Working in batches, air-fry the meatballs for 8 minutes, turning the meatballs over halfway through the cooking time. Drizzle some of the Thai sweet chili sauce on top of each meatball and return the basket to the air fryer, air-frying for another 2 minutes. Reserve the remaining Thai sweet chili sauce for serving.

4. As soon as the meatballs are done, sprinkle with toasted sesame seeds and transfer them to a serving platter. Scatter the scallions around and serve warm.

Lamb Burgers

Servings: 3
Cooking Time: 17 Minutes
Ingredients:
- 1 pound 2 ounces Ground lamb
- 3 tablespoons Crumbled feta
- 1 teaspoon Minced garlic
- 1 teaspoon Tomato paste
- ¾ teaspoon Ground coriander
- ¾ teaspoon Ground dried ginger
- Up to ⅛ teaspoon Cayenne
- Up to a ⅛ teaspoon Table salt (optional)
- 3 Kaiser rolls or hamburger buns (gluten-free, if a concern), split open

Directions:
1. Preheat the air fryer to 375°F .
2. Gently mix the ground lamb, feta, garlic, tomato paste, coriander, ginger, cayenne, and salt (if using) in a bowl until well combined, trying to keep the bits of cheese intact. Form this mixture into two 5-inch patties for the small batch, three 5-inch patties for the medium, or four 5-inch patties for the large.
3. Set the patties in the basket in one layer and air-fry undisturbed for 16 minutes, or until an instant-read meat thermometer inserted into one burger registers 160°F. (The cheese is not an issue with the temperature probe in this recipe as it was for the Inside-Out Cheeseburgers, because the feta is so well mixed into the ground meat.)
4. Use a nonstick-safe spatula, and perhaps a flatware fork for balance, to transfer the burgers to a cutting board. Set the buns cut side down in the basket in one layer (working in batches as necessary) and air-fry undisturbed for 1 minute, to toast a bit and warm up. Serve the burgers warm in the buns.

Salmon Burgers

Servings: 3

Cooking Time: 8 Minutes

Ingredients:

- 1 pound 2 ounces Skinless salmon fillet, preferably fattier Atlantic salmon
- 1½ tablespoons Minced chives or the green part of a scallion
- ½ cup Plain panko bread crumbs (gluten-free, if a concern)
- 1½ teaspoons Dijon mustard (gluten-free, if a concern)
- 1½ teaspoons Drained and rinsed capers, minced
- 1½ teaspoons Lemon juice
- ¼ teaspoon Table salt
- ¼ teaspoon Ground black pepper
- Vegetable oil spray

Directions:

1. Preheat the air fryer to 375°F .

2. Cut the salmon into pieces that will fit in a food processor. Cover and pulse until coarsely chopped. Add the chives and pulse to combine, until the fish is ground but not a paste. Scrape down and remove the blade. Scrape the salmon mixture into a bowl. Add the bread crumbs, mustard, capers, lemon juice, salt, and pepper. Stir gently until well combined.

3. Use clean and dry hands to form the mixture into two 5-inch patties for a small batch, three 5-inch patties for a medium batch, or four 5-inch patties for a large one.

4. Coat both sides of each patty with vegetable oil spray. Set them in the basket in one layer and air-fry undisturbed for 8 minutes, or until browned and an instant-read meat thermometer inserted into the center of a burger registers 145°F.

5. Use a nonstick-safe spatula, and perhaps a flatware fork for balance, to transfer the burgers to a wire rack. Cool for 2 or 3 minutes before serving.

Chicken Gyros

Servings: 4
Cooking Time: 14 Minutes
Ingredients:

- 4 4- to 5-ounce boneless skinless chicken thighs, trimmed of any fat blobs
- 2 tablespoons Lemon juice
- 2 tablespoons Red wine vinegar
- 2 tablespoons Olive oil
- 2 teaspoons Dried oregano
- 2 teaspoons Minced garlic
- 1 teaspoon Table salt
- 1 teaspoon Ground black pepper
- 4 Pita pockets (gluten-free, if a concern)
- ½ cup Chopped tomatoes
- ½ cup Bottled regular, low-fat, or fat-free ranch dressing (gluten-free, if a concern)

Directions:

1. Mix the thighs, lemon juice, vinegar, oil, oregano, garlic, salt, and pepper in a zip-closed bag. Seal, gently massage the marinade into the meat through the plastic, and refrigerate for at least 2 hours or up to 6 hours. (Longer than that and the meat can turn rubbery.)

2. Set the plastic bag out on the counter (to make the contents a little less frigid). Preheat the air fryer to 375°F .

3. When the machine is at temperature, use kitchen tongs to place the thighs in the basket in one layer. Discard the marinade. Air-fry the chicken thighs undisturbed for 12 minutes, or until browned and an instant-read meat thermometer inserted into the thickest part of one thigh registers 165°F. You may need to air-fry the chicken 2 minutes longer if the machine's temperature is 360°F.

4. Use kitchen tongs to transfer the thighs to a cutting board. Cool for 5 minutes, then set one thigh in each of the pita pockets. Top each with 2 tablespoons chopped tomatoes and 2 tablespoons dressing. Serve warm.

Inside Out Cheeseburgers

Servings: 2
Cooking Time: 20 Minutes
Ingredients:
- ¾ pound lean ground beef
- 3 tablespoons minced onion
- 4 teaspoons ketchup
- 2 teaspoons yellow mustard
- salt and freshly ground black pepper
- 4 slices of Cheddar cheese, broken into smaller pieces
- 8 hamburger dill pickle chips

Directions:
1. Combine the ground beef, minced onion, ketchup, mustard, salt and pepper in a large bowl. Mix well to thoroughly combine the ingredients. Divide the meat into four equal portions.
2. To make the stuffed burgers, flatten each portion of meat into a thin patty. Place 4 pickle chips and half of the cheese onto the center of two of the patties, leaving a rim around the edge of the patty exposed. Place the remaining two patties on top of the first and press the meat together firmly, sealing the edges tightly. With the burgers on a flat surface, press the sides of the burger with the palm of your hand to create a straight edge. This will help keep the stuffing inside the burger while it cooks.
3. Preheat the air fryer to 370°F.
4. Place the burgers inside the air fryer basket and air-fry for 20 minutes, flipping the burgers over halfway through the cooking time.
5. Serve the cheeseburgers on buns with lettuce and tomato.

Reuben Sandwiches

Servings: 2

Cooking Time: 11 Minutes

Ingredients:

- ½ pound Sliced deli corned beef
- 4 teaspoons Regular or low-fat mayonnaise (not fat-free)
- 4 Rye bread slices
- 2 tablespoons plus 2 teaspoons Russian dressing
- ½ cup Purchased sauerkraut, squeezed by the handful over the sink to get rid of excess moisture
- 2 ounces (2 to 4 slices) Swiss cheese slices (optional)

Directions:

1. Set the corned beef in the basket, slip the basket into the machine, and heat the air fryer to 400°F. Air-fry undisturbed for 3 minutes from the time the basket is put in the machine, just to warm up the meat.

2. Use kitchen tongs to transfer the corned beef to a cutting board. Spread 1 teaspoon mayonnaise on one side of each slice of rye bread, rubbing the mayonnaise into the bread with a small flatware knife.

3. Place the bread slices mayonnaise side down on a cutting board. Spread the Russian dressing over the "dry" side of each slice. For one sandwich, top one slice of bread with the corned beef, sauerkraut, and cheese (if using). For two sandwiches, top two slices of bread each with half of the corned beef, sauerkraut, and cheese (if using). Close the sandwiches with the remaining bread, setting it mayonnaise side up on top.

4. Set the sandwich(es) in the basket and air-fry undisturbed for 8 minutes, or until browned and crunchy.

5. Use a nonstick-safe spatula, and perhaps a flatware fork for balance, to transfer the sandwich(es) to a cutting board. Cool for 2 or 3 minutes before slicing in half and serving.

Mexican Cheeseburgers

Servings: 4
Cooking Time: 22 Minutes
Ingredients:

- 1¼ pounds ground beef
- ¼ cup finely chopped onion
- ½ cup crushed yellow corn tortilla chips
- 1 (1.25-ounce) packet taco seasoning
- ¼ cup canned diced green chilies
- 1 egg, lightly beaten
- 4 ounces pepper jack cheese, grated
- 4 (12-inch) flour tortillas
- shredded lettuce, sour cream, guacamole, salsa (for topping)

Directions:

1. Combine the ground beef, minced onion, crushed tortilla chips, taco seasoning, green chilies, and egg in a large bowl. Mix thoroughly until combined – your hands are good tools for this. Divide the meat into four equal portions and shape each portion into an oval-shaped burger.

2. Preheat the air fryer to 370°F.

3. Air-fry the burgers for 18 minutes, turning them over halfway through the cooking time. Divide the cheese between the burgers, lower fryer to 340°F and air-fry for an additional 4 minutes to melt the cheese. (This will give you a burger that is medium-well. If you prefer your cheeseburger medium-rare, shorten the cooking time to about 15 minutes and then add the cheese and proceed with the recipe.)

4. While the burgers are cooking, warm the tortillas wrapped in aluminum foil in a 350°F oven, or in a skillet with a little oil over medium-high heat for a couple of minutes. Keep the tortillas warm until the burgers are ready.

5. To assemble the burgers, spread sour cream over three quarters of the tortillas and top each with some shredded lettuce and salsa. Place the Mexican cheeseburgers on the lettuce and top with guacamole. Fold the tortillas around the burger, starting with the bottom and then folding the sides in over the top. (A little sour cream can help hold the seam of the tortilla together.) Serve immediately.

Desserts And Sweets
Grilled Pineapple Dessert

Servings: 4
Cooking Time: 12 Minutes
Ingredients:

- oil for misting or cooking spray
- 4 ½-inch-thick slices fresh pineapple, core removed
- 1 tablespoon honey
- ¼ teaspoon brandy
- 2 tablespoons slivered almonds, toasted
- vanilla frozen yogurt or coconut sorbet

Directions:
1. Spray both sides of pineapple slices with oil or cooking spray. Place on grill plate or directly into air fryer basket.
2. Cook at 390°F for 6minutes. Turn slices over and cook for an additional 6minutes.
3. Mix together the honey and brandy.
4. Remove cooked pineapple slices from air fryer, sprinkle with toasted almonds, and drizzle with honey mixture.
5. Serve with a scoop of frozen yogurt or sorbet on the side.

Rustic Berry Layer Cake

Servings: 6
Cooking Time: 45 Minutes
Ingredients:

- 2 eggs, beaten
- ½ cup milk
- 2 tbsp Greek yogurt
- ¼ cup maple syrup
- 1 tbsp apple cider vinegar
- 1 tbsp vanilla extract
- ¾ cup all-purpose flour
- 1 tsp baking powder
- ½ tsp baking soda
- ¼ cup dark chocolate chips
- 1/3 cup raspberry jam

Directions:
1. Preheat air fryer to 350°F. Combine the eggs, milk, Greek yogurt, maple syrup, apple vinegar, and vanilla extract in a bowl. Toss in flour, baking powder, and baking soda until combined. Pour the batter into a 6-inch round cake pan, distributing well, and Bake for 20-25 minutes until a toothpick comes out clean. Let cool completely.
2. Turn the cake onto a plate, cut lengthwise to make 2 equal layers. Set aside. Add chocolate chips to a heat-proof bowl and Bake for 3 minutes until fully melted. In the meantime, spread raspberry jam on top of the bottom layer, distributing well, and top with the remaining layer. Once the chocolate is ready, stir in 1 tbsp of milk. Pour over the layer cake and spread well. Cut into 6 wedges and serve immediately.

Almond-roasted Pears

Servings: 4
Cooking Time: 15 Minutes
Ingredients:

- Yogurt Topping
- 1 container vanilla Greek yogurt (5–6 ounces)
- ¼ teaspoon almond flavoring
- 2 whole pears
- ¼ cup crushed Biscoff cookies (approx. 4 cookies)
- 1 tablespoon sliced almonds
- 1 tablespoon butter

Directions:

1. Stir almond flavoring into yogurt and set aside while preparing pears.
2. Halve each pear and spoon out the core.
3. Place pear halves in air fryer basket.
4. Stir together the cookie crumbs and almonds. Place a quarter of this mixture into the hollow of each pear half.
5. Cut butter into 4 pieces and place one piece on top of crumb mixture in each pear.
6. Cook at 360°F for 15 minutes or until pears have cooked through but are still slightly firm.
7. Serve pears warm with a dollop of yogurt topping.

Coconut-custard Pie

Servings: 4
Cooking Time: 20 Minutes
Ingredients:

- 1 cup milk
- ¼ cup plus 2 tablespoons sugar
- ¼ cup biscuit baking mix
- 1 teaspoon vanilla
- 2 eggs
- 2 tablespoons melted butter
- cooking spray
- ½ cup shredded, sweetened coconut

Directions:

1. Place all ingredients except coconut in a medium bowl.
2. Using a hand mixer, beat on high speed for 3minutes.
3. Let sit for 5minutes.
4. Preheat air fryer to 330°F.
5. Spray a 6-inch round or 6 x 6-inch square baking pan with cooking spray and place pan in air fryer basket.
6. Pour filling into pan and sprinkle coconut over top.
7. Cook pie at 330°F for 20 minutes or until center sets.

Baked Stuffed Pears

Servings: 4
Cooking Time: 15 Minutes + Cooling Time
Ingredients:

- 4 cored pears, halved
- ½ cup chopped cashews
- ½ cup dried cranberries
- ¼ cup agave nectar
- ½ stick butter, softened
- ½ tsp ground cinnamon
- ½ cup apple juice

Directions:
1. Preheat the air fryer to 350°F. Combine the cashews, cranberries, agave nectar, butter, and cinnamon and mix well. Stuff this mixture into the pears, heaping it up on top. Set the pears in a baking pan and pour the apple juice into the bottom of the pan. Put the pan in the fryer and Bake for 10-12 minutes or until the pears are tender. Let cool before serving.

Gingerbread

Servings: 6
Cooking Time: 20 Minutes
Ingredients:

- cooking spray
- 1 cup flour
- 2 tablespoons sugar
- ¾ teaspoon ground ginger
- ¼ teaspoon cinnamon
- 1 teaspoon baking powder
- ½ teaspoon baking soda
- ⅛ teaspoon salt
- 1 egg
- ¼ cup molasses
- ½ cup buttermilk
- 2 tablespoons oil
- 1 teaspoon pure vanilla extract

Directions:
1. Preheat air fryer to 330°F.
2. Spray 6 x 6-inch baking dish lightly with cooking spray.
3. In a medium bowl, mix together all the dry ingredients.
4. In a separate bowl, beat the egg. Add molasses, buttermilk, oil, and vanilla and stir until well mixed.
5. Pour liquid mixture into dry ingredients and stir until well blended.
6. Pour batter into baking dish and cook at 330°F for 20minutes or until toothpick inserted in center of loaf comes out clean.

Boston Cream Donut Holes

Servings: 24
Cooking Time: 12 Minutes
Ingredients:

- 1½ cups bread flour
- 1 teaspoon active dry yeast
- 1 tablespoon sugar
- ¼ teaspoon salt
- ½ cup warm milk
- ½ teaspoon pure vanilla extract
- 2 egg yolks
- 2 tablespoons butter, melted
- vegetable oil
- Custard Filling:
- 1 (3.4-ounce) box French vanilla instant pudding mix
- ¾ cup whole milk
- ¼ cup heavy cream
- Chocolate Glaze:
- 1 cup chocolate chips
- ⅓ cup heavy cream

Directions:

1. Combine the flour, yeast, sugar and salt in the bowl of a stand mixer. Add the milk, vanilla, egg yolks and butter. Mix until the dough starts to come together in a ball. Transfer the dough to a floured surface and knead the dough by hand for 2 minutes. Shape the dough into a ball, place it in a large oiled bowl, cover the bowl with a clean kitchen towel and let the dough rise for 1 to 1½ hours or until the dough has doubled in size.

2. When the dough has risen, punch it down and roll it into a 24-inch log. Cut the dough into 24 pieces and roll each piece into a ball. Place the dough balls on a baking sheet and let them rise for another 30 minutes.

3. Preheat the air fryer to 400°F.

4. Spray or brush the dough balls lightly with vegetable oil and air-fry eight at a time for 4 minutes, turning them over halfway through the cooking time.

5. While donut holes are cooking, make the filling and chocolate glaze. To make the filling, use an electric hand mixer to beat the French vanilla pudding, milk and ¼ cup of heavy cream together for 2 minutes.

6. To make the chocolate glaze, place the chocolate chips in a medium-sized bowl. Bring the heavy cream to a boil on the stovetop and pour it over the chocolate chips. Stir until the chips are melted and the glaze is smooth.

7. To fill the donut holes, place the custard filling in a pastry bag with a long tip. Poke a hole into the side of the donut hole with a small knife. Wiggle the knife around to make room for the filling. Place the pastry bag tip into the hole and slowly squeeze the custard into the center of the donut. Dip the top half of the donut into the chocolate glaze, letting any excess glaze drip back into the bowl. Let the glazed donut holes sit for a few minutes before serving.

Guilty Chocolate Cookies

Servings: 6
Cooking Time: 25 Minutes
Ingredients:

- 3 eggs, beaten
- 1 tsp vanilla extract
- 1 tsp apple cider vinegar
- 1/3 cup butter, softened
- 1/3 cup sugar
- ¼ cup cacao powder
- ¼ tsp baking soda

Directions:

1. Preheat air fryer to 300°F. Combine eggs, vanilla extract, and apple vinegar in a bowl until well combined. Refrigerate for 5 minutes. Whisk in butter and sugar until smooth, finally toss in cacao powder and baking soda until smooth. Make balls out of the mixture. Place the balls onto the parchment-lined frying basket. Bake for 13 minutes until brown. Using a fork, flatten each cookie. Let cool completely before serving.

Thumbprint Sugar Cookies

Servings: 10
Cooking Time: 8 Minutes
Ingredients:

- 2½ tablespoons butter
- ⅓ cup cane sugar
- 1 teaspoon pure vanilla extract
- 1 large egg
- 1 cup all-purpose flour
- ½ teaspoon baking soda
- ¼ teaspoon salt
- 10 chocolate kisses

Directions:

1. Preheat the air fryer to 350°F.
2. In a large bowl, cream the butter with the sugar and vanilla. Whisk in the egg and set aside.
3. In a separate bowl, mix the flour, baking soda, and salt. Then gently mix the dry ingredients into the wet. Portion the dough into 10 balls; then press down on each with the bottom of a cup to create a flat cookie.
4. Liberally spray the metal trivet of an air fryer basket with olive oil mist.
5. Place the cookies in the air fryer basket on the trivet and cook for 8 minutes or until the tops begin to lightly brown.
6. Remove and immediately press the chocolate kisses into the tops of the cookies while still warm.
7. Let cool 5 minutes and then enjoy.

Orange Gooey Butter Cake

Servings: 6
Cooking Time: 85 Minutes
Ingredients:
- Crust Layer:
- ½ cup flour
- ¼ cup sugar
- ½ teaspoon baking powder
- ⅛ teaspoon salt
- 2 ounces (½ stick) unsalted European style butter, melted
- 1 egg
- 1 teaspoon orange extract
- 2 tablespoons orange zest
- Gooey Butter Layer:
- 8 ounces cream cheese, softened
- 4 ounces (1 stick) unsalted European style butter, melted
- 2 eggs
- 2 teaspoons orange extract
- 2 tablespoons orange zest
- 4 cups powdered sugar
- Garnish:
- powdered sugar
- orange slices

Directions:
1. Preheat the air fryer to 350°F.
2. Grease a 7-inch cake pan and line the bottom with parchment paper. Combine the flour, sugar, baking powder and salt in a bowl. Add the melted butter, egg, orange extract and orange zest. Mix well and press this mixture into the bottom of the greased cake pan. Lower the pan into the basket using an aluminum foil sling (fold a piece of aluminum foil into a strip about 2-inches wide by 24-inches long). Fold the ends of the aluminum foil over the top of the dish before returning the basket to the air fryer. Air-fry uncovered for 8 minutes.
3. To make the gooey butter layer, beat the cream cheese, melted butter, eggs, orange extract and orange zest in a large bowl using an electric hand mixer. Add the powdered sugar in stages, beat until smooth with each addition. Pour this mixture on top of the baked crust in the cake pan. Wrap the pan with a piece of greased aluminum foil, tenting the top of the foil to leave a little room for the cake to rise.
4. Air-fry for 60 minutes at 350°F. Remove the aluminum foil and air-fry for an additional 17 minutes.
5. Let the cake cool inside the pan for at least 10 minutes. Then, run a butter knife around the cake and let the cake cool completely in the pan. When cooled, run the butter knife around the edges of the cake again and invert it onto a plate and then back onto a serving platter. Sprinkle the powdered sugar over the top of the cake and garnish with orange slices.

Strawberry Pastry Rolls

Servings: 4
Cooking Time: 6 Minutes
Ingredients:

- 3 ounces low-fat cream cheese
- 2 tablespoons plain yogurt
- 2 teaspoons sugar
- ¼ teaspoon pure vanilla extract
- 8 ounces fresh strawberries
- 8 sheets phyllo dough
- butter-flavored cooking spray
- ¼–½ cup dark chocolate chips (optional)

Directions:

1. In a medium bowl, combine the cream cheese, yogurt, sugar, and vanilla. Beat with hand mixer at high speed until smooth, about 1 minute.
2. Wash strawberries and destem. Chop enough of them to measure ½ cup. Stir into cheese mixture.
3. Preheat air fryer to 330°F.
4. Phyllo dough dries out quickly, so cover your stack of phyllo sheets with waxed paper and then place a damp dish towel on top of that. Remove only one sheet at a time as you work.
5. To create one pastry roll, lay out a single sheet of phyllo. Spray lightly with butter-flavored spray, top with a second sheet of phyllo, and spray the second sheet lightly.
6. Place a quarter of the filling (about 3 tablespoons) about ½ inch from the edge of one short side. Fold the end of the phyllo over the filling and keep rolling a turn or two. Fold in both the left and right sides so that the edges meet in the middle of your roll. Then roll up completely. Spray outside of pastry roll with butter spray.
7. When you have 4 rolls, place them in the air fryer basket, seam side down, leaving some space in between each. Cook at 330°F for 6 minutes, until they turn a delicate golden brown.
8. Repeat step 7 for remaining rolls.
9. Allow pastries to cool to room temperature.
10. When ready to serve, slice the remaining strawberries. If desired, melt the chocolate chips in microwave or double boiler. Place 1 pastry on each dessert plate, and top with sliced strawberries. Drizzle melted chocolate over strawberries and onto plate.

One-bowl Chocolate Buttermilk Cake

Servings: 6
Cooking Time: 16-20 Minutes
Ingredients:

- ¾ cup All-purpose flour
- ½ cup Granulated white sugar
- 3 tablespoons Unsweetened cocoa powder
- ½ teaspoon Baking soda
- ¼ teaspoon Table salt
- ½ cup Buttermilk
- 2 tablespoons Vegetable oil
- ¾ teaspoon Vanilla extract
- Baking spray (see here)

Directions:

1. Preheat the air fryer to 325°F (or 330°F, if that's the closest setting).
2. Stir the flour, sugar, cocoa powder, baking soda, and salt in a large bowl until well combined. Add the buttermilk, oil, and vanilla. Stir just until a thick, grainy batter forms.
3. Use the baking spray to generously coat the inside of a 6-inch round cake pan for a small batch, a 7-inch round cake pan for a medium batch, or an 8-inch round cake pan for a large batch. Scrape and spread the chocolate batter into this pan, smoothing the batter out to an even layer.
4. Set the pan in the basket and air-fry undisturbed for 16 minutes for a 6-inch layer, 18 minutes for a 7-inch layer, or 20 minutes for an 8-inch layer, or until a toothpick or cake tester inserted into the center of the cake comes out clean. Start checking it at the 14-minute mark to know where you are.
5. Use hot pads or silicone baking mitts to transfer the cake pan to a wire rack. Cool for 5 minutes. To unmold, set a cutting board over the baking pan and invert both the board and the pan. Lift the still-warm pan off the cake layer. Set the wire rack on top of the cake layer and invert all of it with the cutting board so that the cake layer is now right side up on the wire rack. Remove the cutting board and continue cooling the cake for at least 10 minutes or to room temperature, about 30 minutes, before slicing into wedges.

Oatmeal Blackberry Crisp

Servings: 6
Cooking Time: 20 Minutes
Ingredients:

- 1 cup rolled oats
- ½ cup flour
- ¼ cup olive oil
- ¼ tsp salt
- 1 tsp cinnamon
- 1/3 cup honey
- 4 cups blackberries

Directions:

1. Preheat air fryer to 350°F. Combine rolled oats, flour, olive oil, salt, cinnamon, and honey in a large bowl. Mix well. Spread blackberries on the bottom of a greased cooking pan. Cover them with the oat mixture. Place pan in air fryer and Bake for 15 minutes. Cool for a few minutes. Serve and enjoy.

Baked Caramelized Peaches

Servings: 6
Cooking Time: 25 Minutes
Ingredients:
- 3 pitted peaches, halved
- 2 tbsp brown sugar
- 1 cup heavy cream
- 1 tsp vanilla extract
- ¼ tsp ground cinnamon
- 1 cup fresh blueberries

Directions:
1. Preheat air fryer to 380°F. Lay the peaches in the frying basket with the cut side up, then top them with brown sugar. Bake for 7-11 minutes, allowing the peaches to brown around the edges. In a mixing bowl, whisk heavy cream, vanilla, and cinnamon until stiff peaks form. Fold the peaches into a plate. Spoon the cream mixture into the peach cups, top with blueberries, and serve.

Date Oat Cookies

Servings: 6
Cooking Time: 20 Minutes
Ingredients:
- ¼ cup butter, softened
- 2 ½ tbsp milk
- ½ cup sugar
- ½ tsp vanilla extract
- ½ tsp lemon zest
- ½ tsp ground cinnamon
- 3/4 cup flour
- ¼ tsp salt
- ¾ cup rolled oats
- ¼ tsp baking soda
- ¼ tsp baking powder
- 2 tbsp dates, chopped

Directions:
1. Use an electric beater to whip the butter until fluffy. Add the milk, sugar, lemon zest, and vanilla. Stir until well combined. Add the cinnamon, flour, salt, oats, baking soda, and baking powder in a separate bowl and stir. Add the dry mix to the wet mix and stir with a wooden spoon. Pour in the dates.
2. Preheat air fryer to 350°F. Drop tablespoonfuls of the batter onto a greased baking pan, leaving room in between each. Bake for 6 minutes or until light brown. Make all the cookies at once, or save the batter in the fridge for later. Let them cool and enjoy!

Giant Oatmeal-peanut Butter Cookie

Servings: 4

Cooking Time: 18 Minutes

Ingredients:

- 1 cup Rolled oats (not quick-cooking or steel-cut oats)
- ½ cup All-purpose flour
- ½ teaspoon Ground cinnamon
- ½ teaspoon Baking soda
- ⅓ cup Packed light brown sugar
- ¼ cup Solid vegetable shortening
- 2 tablespoons Natural-style creamy peanut butter
- 3 tablespoons Granulated white sugar
- 2 tablespoons (or 1 small egg, well beaten) Pasteurized egg substitute, such as Egg Beaters
- ⅓ cup Roasted, salted peanuts, chopped
- Baking spray

Directions:

1. Preheat the air fryer to 350°F .

2. Stir the oats, flour, cinnamon, and baking soda in a bowl until well combined.

3. Using an electric hand mixer at medium speed, beat the brown sugar, shortening, peanut butter, granulated white sugar, and egg substitute or egg (as applicable) until smooth and creamy, about 3 minutes, scraping down the inside of the bowl occasionally.

4. Scrape down and remove the beaters. Fold in the flour mixture and peanuts with a rubber spatula just until all the flour is moistened and the peanut bits are evenly distributed in the dough.

5. For a small air fryer, coat the inside of a 6-inch round cake pan with baking spray. For a medium air fryer, coat the inside of a 7-inch round cake pan with baking spray. And for a large air fryer, coat the inside of an 8-inch round cake pan with baking spray. Scrape and gently press the dough into the prepared pan, spreading it into an even layer to the perimeter.

6. Set the pan in the basket and air-fry undisturbed for 18 minutes, or until well browned.

7. Transfer the pan to a wire rack and cool for 15 minutes. Loosen the cookie from the perimeter with a spatula, then invert the pan onto a cutting board and let the cookie come free. Remove the pan and reinvert the cookie onto the wire rack. Cool for 5 minutes more before slicing into wedges to serve.

Party S´mores

Servings: 6
Cooking Time: 15 Minutes
Ingredients:
- 2 dark chocolate bars, cut into 12 pieces
- 12 buttermilk biscuits
- 12 marshmallows

Directions:
1. Preheat air fryer to 350°F. Place 6 biscuits in the air fryer. Top each square with a piece of dark chocolate. Bake for 2 minutes. Add a marshmallow to each piece of chocolate. Cook for another minute. Remove and top with another piece of biscuit. Serve warm.

Pecan-oat Filled Apples

Servings: 4
Cooking Time: 20 Minutes
Ingredients:
- 2 cored Granny Smith apples, halved
- ¼ cup rolled oats
- 2 tbsp honey
- ½ tsp ground cinnamon
- ½ tsp ground ginger
- 2 tbsp chopped pecans
- A pinch of salt
- 1 tbsp olive oil

Directions:
1. Preheat air fryer to 380°F. Combine together the oats, honey, cinnamon, ginger, pecans, salt, and olive oil in a bowl. Scoop a quarter of the oat mixture onto the top of each half apple. Put the apples in the frying basket and Roast for 12-15 minutes until the apples are fork-tender.

Spiced Fruit Skewers

Servings: 4
Cooking Time: 15 Minutes
Ingredients:

- 2 peeled peaches, thickly sliced
- 3 plums, halved and pitted
- 3 peeled kiwi, quartered
- 1 tbsp honey
- ½ tsp ground cinnamon
- ¼ tsp ground allspice
- ¼ tsp cayenne pepper

Directions:
1. Preheat air fryer to 400°F. Combine the honey, cinnamon, allspice, and cayenne and set aside. Alternate fruits on 8 bamboo skewers, then brush the fruit with the honey mix. Lay the skewers in the air fryer and Air Fry for 3-5 minutes. Allow to chill for 5 minutes before serving.

Homemade Chips Ahoy

Servings: 4
Cooking Time: 20 Minutes
Ingredients:

- 1 tbsp coconut oil, melted
- 1 tbsp honey
- 1 tbsp milk
- ½ tsp vanilla extract
- ¼ cup oat flour
- 2 tbsp coconut sugar
- ¼ tsp salt
- ¼ tsp baking powder
- 2 tbsp chocolate chips

Directions:
1. Combine the coconut oil, honey, milk, and vanilla in a bowl. Add the oat flour, coconut sugar, salt, and baking powder. Stir until combined. Add the chocolate chips and stir. Preheat air fryer to 350°F. Pour the batter into a greased baking pan, leaving a little room in between. Bake for 7 minutes or until golden. Do not overcook. Move to a cooling rack and serve chilled.

INDEX

Printed in Great Britain
by Amazon

38513413R00066